All My Young Years

Yiddish Poetry
from Weimar Germany

In Memory of
Majer Bogdanski
(1912–2005)

All My Young Years

Yiddish Poetry from Weimar Germany

A.N. Stencl

Translated by
Haike Beruriah Wiegand
and Stephen Watts

Introduction by Heather Valencia

Five Leaves Publications

www.fiveleaves.co.uk

All My Young Years
Yiddish Poetry from Weimar Germany
A.N. Stencl

Published in 2007 by Five Leaves Publications
PO Box 8786 Nottingham, NG1 9AW
info@fiveleaves.co.uk, www.fiveleaves.co.uk

Five Leaves acknowledge financial assistance from
Arts Council England

Five Leaves is a member of Inpress
(www.inpress.co.uk)
representing independent publishers.

ISBN: 978-1-905512-23-2

Typeset and designed by
Four Sheets Design and Print
Yiddish typesetting by Haike Beruriah Wiegand
Printed and bound in Great Britain

Contents

A.N. Stencl, 1932
(By permission of Archiv Bibliographica Judaica)

A.N. Stencl

Avrom Nokhem Stencl was born in 1897 in the town of Czeladz, near Sosnowiec, in south-western Poland. He grew up in a religious family from the Jewish Hassidic tradition.[1] Though Stencl later felt himself to be cut off from his religious heritage, his Hassidic background was a strong influence on his earlier poetry.

Ancestry was extremely important to the traditional Eastern European Jews, and Stencl's family background was impeccable: his paternal grandfather was the *dayan,* (the judge of a religious court) in the town of Częstochowa, and his maternal grandfather was the first Jew to settle in Czeladz. The latter's economic success enabled his son-in-law to study, and Stencl's father became a scholar of Talmud and Kabbala, and the rabbi of the small Jewish community in the town. Stencl studied first with his father and then at the *yeshiva* (Talmudic academy) of Sosnowiec, where his older brother Shloyme was the rabbi. He later lived in Częstochowa, where he was active in a Zionist group. In Stencl's teenage years a friend introduced him to Yiddish literature, and Stencl began writing poetry in Yiddish.

This was a significant step in the young man's life, for modern Yiddish literature was suspect in religious Jewish households. For observant Jews in Eastern Europe, two languages played a role in their lives. Hebrew, known as *loshn koydesh* — the holy tongue — was reserved principally for the sphere of religion. The sacred writings, and prayers were in Hebrew with some Aramaic,[2] while Yiddish was then the spoken language of every day. Literature in both languages had always existed, but was predominantly religious, and Yiddish literature was written principally with the female reader in mind. From the mid-nineteenth century, modern literature in Yiddish began to flourish in Poland and Russia. It was regarded by traditional religious Jews as purveying dangerous secular ideas.

Stencl's early literary activities were therefore a source of inner conflict. Like many other Yiddish writers of that time, he struggled in his memoirs and poetry to reconcile traditional religious teaching with modern literary individualism, and to justify to himself his rupture with the world of his parents and grandparents. In his memoirs he captures this dualism in his characterisation of himself as a young Hassid with skullcap and sidelocks, the pockets of his traditional gabardine stuffed with bundles of papers covered with poems.

In 1919 Stencl was called up to the Polish army and immediately fled to Holland, apparently with the blessing and active help of his father and his brother, the rabbi of Sosnowiec.[3] Stencl never returned to Poland, and it seems that he never saw his parents again. Most of his family were wiped out in the Holocaust, but his one brother had two surviving sons: one moved to England, in 1936, the other lived in Israel.

In Holland he worked in an iron foundry and as an agricultural labourer, and in 1921 crossed the border into Germany. He lived mainly in Berlin, but with periods in Leipzig, in the Harz mountains, in the countryside round Berlin, and on the Wolin peninsula on the Baltic coast.[4] By 1936 most of the Jewish artists and writers had left Germany, but Stencl still remained. In his memoirs he himself laconically cites his "lethargy" as the reason he stayed so long, but his close relationship with the German teacher Elisabeth Wöhler must certainly have played a role in his unwillingness to go.[5] However, when he was notified that as a member of the German Writers' Association he would henceforth have to wear a swastika lapel-badge, he decided that the time had come to leave.[6] Christobel Fowler-Sinsheimer, an English Quaker, who was married to the director of the Munich *Kammerspiele* Theatre, was at that time helping Jews to escape from Germany, and she procured a visa for him to enter Britain in order to research an essay on English painting. Stencl left Germany in November 1936, and settled in London's Jewish district of Whitechapel, where he remained till his death in 1983.

Berlin as a centre of Yiddish culture

In the early twenties there were 200,000 Jews in Berlin. By 1925, nearly a quarter of these were foreign Jews, the vast majority from Eastern Europe. Many had fled the aftermath of the First World War and the Russian Revolution. Yiddish-speaking intellectuals and writers were drawn to Berlin, which was the foremost centre of the literary and artistic avant-garde in the early years of the twentieth century.

A crucial aspect of this literary activity was the flourishing of Yiddish publishing in the Weimar Republic in the early 1920s. German inflation meant that publishers paying in foreign currency could afford to set up businesses in Germany. Yiddish literature was flourishing in the young Soviet Union and newly independent Poland. The expansion of secular Yiddish-language schools there created a lively market for Yiddish books. These began to be published in Berlin, as new presses were established and a number of existing East European firms opened branches there. The successful German Ullstein Verlag established a Yiddish press, the Klal Farlag, publishing beautiful editions of Yiddish literary texts. There were important journals too, including *Der Mizrakh-yud* (The Eastern Jew) and a magnificent art journal in a Hebrew and Yiddish edition, entitled *Rimon* and *Milgroym* respectively.[7] The lack of censorship in the Weimar Republic enabled material to be published which would have been inadmissable in Eastern Europe. Thus, for example, the poet Uri-Zvi Grinberg's avant-garde literary journal *Albatros*, which had been banned in Warsaw for blasphemy,[8] appeared in Berlin in 1923.

The Yiddish writers and artists frequented the Romanische Café, one of the principal meeting-places of the cultural élite. As Walter Laqueur puts it: "Avant-garde and mass culture met in the coffee houses such as the Romanische Café, at the corner of Tauentzien and Budapester Strasse, a stone's throw from the Gedächtniskirche [the Kaiser Wilhelm Memorial Church]; there you could see writers and critics, painters and actresses, and quite a few original characters who never published a book, drew a line or composed a sonata, but nevertheless had some influence on contemporary literature, music and painting... School reformers were sitting there next to all kinds of fanatics, revolutionaries next to pickpockets, people on drugs next to apostles of health-food and vegetarianism. Such a mixture caused a great deal of confusion, but it also acted as a strong stimulant."[9]

Stencl underlines the important role this café played in the lives of the Yiddish intellectuals and political activists:

> *Fun di antrunene fun di pogromen in di yidish-ukraynishe shtetlekh, fun groysn hunger in di rusishe shtet un fun di antlofene fun der revolutsye, hot zikh beyneleveyne in vestn fun Berlin geshafn a min yidishe kolonye un dos Romanishe Kafe iz geven der parlament. Es hot geroysht mit barimte yidishe kultur- un klal-tuer, mit bavuste advokatn, yidishe, fun Moskve un Peterburg, mit bakante yidishe shrayber fun Kiev un Odes, mit bafliglte partey-firer funem ekst link biz same rekhtstn fligl — es hot geroysht vi in a binshtok.*
>
> (From those fleeing the pogroms in the Jewish shtetls of the Ukraine, the famine in the Russian cities, or the Revolution, a kind of Jewish colony had meanwhile formed itself in the west of Berlin, and the Romanische Café was its parliament. It buzzed with famous Yiddish intellectuals and activists, with prominent Jewish lawyers from Moscow and St. Petersburg, well-known Yiddish writers from Kiev and Odessa, and with flying party-leaders from the furthest left to the extreme right-wing — it buzzed like a beehive.)[10]

Both Stencl and another Yiddish writer, Daniel Charney, use significant images from Jewish religious and folk tradition to convey the significance of Berlin, and in particular of the Romanische Café, for the Eastern European Jewish intellectuals. Charney calls the Berlin of the 1920s an *ir v'eym b'Isroel*, a city and mother in Israel, a Biblical term[11] which has come to designate cities of the diaspora of special importance in Jewish life. Both writers call the Romanische Café a *kibets-golyes*, a phrase signifying the ingathering of Jews from all over the world to the Land of Israel, and by extension used for any refuge where Jews from different places can meet in safety. These images, together with the nickname given to the café, the "Rakhmones Café" ("café of mercy"), indicate in a playful way the importance to these exiles of having an "address" of their own.

Stencl's life in Berlin

It was here that Stencl too found a refuge. He describes many encounters in the Romanische Café, among others the evening on which he first met the famous poet Else Lasker-Schüler, one of his most colourful and eccentric friends from the Berlin period.[12] He was indeed a refugee, having crossed the border between Holland and Germany illegally. This caught up with him in June 1925, when he was sentenced to three months in Berlin's Moabit Prison, of which he served seven weeks.

It is difficult to be specific on exact details of Stencl's life in Germany, as the only narrative source we have are the autobiographical writings in *Loshn un lebn*, which are not chronological, but jump from one event and period to another. Three other testimonies, however, corroborate the general impressions of Stencl's life, personality and relationships which we gain from the memoirs. First, there are the letters which his father sent him from 1921 until the former's death in 1934, in which the parents express their worries about their son's bohemian lifestyle and his infrequent letters home. Second, there are the various letters and postcards sent to him by Else Lasker-Schüler, both before and after her flight from Germany, as well as her poem about Stencl.[13] Finally, there are all the notes and materials collected by or relating to Elisabeth Wöhler, whom Lasker-Schüler referred to as Stencl's "fiancée".[14]

In the early years Stencl seems to have led a hand-to-mouth existence, often sleeping on park benches or on the floors of other Yiddish writers. He depicts himself as an abandoned infant who during the years 1921-1923 could be found lying in any doorway in Berlin.[15] He received some money from his parents, was paid for poems published in newspapers and journals and had various jobs. In his memoirs he mentions, among other things, peddling remnants of material in the suburbs, selling straw hats in a market, starting a business with a partner to manufacture compost from horse dung they collected, and working in a cemetery, stamping down the earth on fresh graves.

Stencl stayed in Germany longer than most other Yiddish writers, and, unlike most, he achieved a considerable literary reputation in German-Jewish circles. Several explanations can be advanced for this. First, Dovid Bergelson, Moyshe Kulbak and the others were already established writers with a reading public in Eastern Europe. They felt their real home to be in the East, and were drawn back there — often with tragic consequences. Stencl, on the other hand, was an unpublished poet whose first works appeared in Germany, and it was there that he made his reputation. Furthermore, he had really burnt his boats: when he left Poland without papers, fleeing from the army, he had forfeited the possibility of return. In a more personal way too, he had cut himself off from his roots. He commented: "Since I had shaved my beard off..., all the bridges to my home had been destroyed."[16] With all that this act symbolised, he had effectively turned his back on the religious tradition of his father and entered secular western society.

Most importantly, the influence of Elisabeth Wöhler on

Stencl's life and literary career was profound. She was a teacher in the *Freie Weltliche Schule* (free secular school) in Reinickendorf, a working-class district of Berlin. This was one of a group of schools established in the early years of the Weimar Republic with an innovative approach to learning and a liberal, secular philosophy. According to Stencl, most of the teachers in this school were socialists and the children were all from poor families. Referring to the worsening political situation in Germany in the early thirties, Stencl remarked in his memoirs: "The teaching in the *Freie Weltliche Schule* made one believe that the world was going forward and that the good in human beings would triumph in the end."[17]

Through the contact with Elisabeth Wöhler, Stencl became familiar with a wider circle of German intellectuals, both Jewish and non-Jewish. She educated him in European art and German literature; at their first meeting — probably in 1924 — she spent the evening reading to him from Goethe's *Faust*. The brief letters she sent to him during his London years are mainly written on picture postcards of paintings they had seen together in Berlin, and allude to the many hours they spent together in art galleries. With regard to German culture, Stencl, by his own admission, had been totally ignorant when he arrived in Germany. He recalls with self-irony how, when embroiled in a conversation about Goethe with his early translator, Abraham Suhl in Leipzig, he betrayed his ignorance and *chutzpah* by challenging Goethe to a poetic duel: "I tell you what, Dr Suhl, you read me a poem by this Goethe and I'll read you one of mine, and we'll see which is better."[18] Through the influence of Elisabeth Wöhler and Else Lasker-Schüler, Stencl, though never learning German very well, came to know a great deal more about both the German classical writers and the contemporary literary scene.

Elisabeth Wöhler made Stencl her life's work. She learnt Yiddish and translated a large selection of his Berlin poetry. Throughout his Berlin years she acted as a literary agent, corresponding with publishers and others on his behalf, and translating or correcting his official letters. Until her death she strove indefatigably to promote his work in Germany and Britain.

It was Elisabeth Wöhler who organised his escape from Germany with the help of Christobel Fowler-Sinsheimer, and in later years she frequently visited him in Whitechapel. Their friendship lasted till Wöhler's death in 1974. Though most of her correspondence preserves the tone of an affectionate old friend, the depth of her feelings for him is touchingly revealed in a note written on her death bed, which is all but indecipherable apart from the heading: "beloved Stencl". She left him most of her money in her will, and after her death Stencl planted 100 trees in her memory in Israel. After her death, a close friend wrote of her: "The world has been impoverished through the death of one of the finest and noblest human beings."[19]

In her later years she painstakingly annotated and ordered the huge mass of papers which Stencl had left with her. She contacted Dr Renate Heuer, the Director of the Archiv Bibliographia Judaica in Frankfurt am Main to ensure that Stencl's legacy should not be forgotten. The archive consists of numerous unpublished manuscripts, translations and letters, as well as papers relating to Elisabeth Wöhler herself. It not only provides a great deal of information about this period in Stencl's life, but also contributes to the discussion of the relationships between German Jews and Eastern European Jews in the early years of the Weimar Republic.

Ostjuden and German Jewry

The success which Stencl's poetry enjoyed among some of the German Jewish intellectuals should be seen against the wider topic of Eastern European Jews in Germany, and the attitudes of German Jewry towards them. The presence in Berlin and other places of large numbers of these Jews who dressed oddly, gesticulated excitedly, and spoke an "outlandish" language which sounded to German ears like a garbled version of their own language, gave rise to prejudiced views of them as dirty, uncivilised beggars who were a burden on the state. The intellectuals from Eastern Europe, on the other hand, dressed more like Westerners, were seen as dangerous radicals.[20]

All this was very uncomfortable for German Jews, many of whose ancestors had themselves been Yiddish-speaking immigrants from the East. The negative reaction of society towards these immigrants seemed, in the eyes of assimilated Jews, to threaten their own hard-won integration in German society. They were ashamed of the foreigners, rather like an upwardly mobile person, who is embarrassed by a poor relative hailing him in the street in front of his new friends in high society. German Jews often distanced themselves from these other Jews, applying against them the prejudices from which they themselves, as Jews, had suffered in German society.

For many German Jews the negative image of the *Ostjude* was also applied to the language: Yiddish was "a target of condescending fun for most German Jews,"[21] or at the very least they were ignorant of the richness of Yiddish literature and culture. Stencl records the surprise of the librarian of the Synagogue on Oranienburgstraße in Berlin as he observes the poet avidly reading Joseph Opatoshu's novel *In poylishe velder* (In Polish Woods): "I am standing here realising that a book in 'jargon' can also be a *seyfer* (a holy book)."[22]

In the course of the nineteen-twenties, however, interesting changes in attitude began to emerge. Many assimilated Jews began to reassess their position in German society in the light of militant nationalism and growing antisemitism. The general climate of uncertainty furthered increasing interest in the Zionist movement, and at the same time a certain modification of attitudes to Eastern European Jews began to develop among German Jewish intellectuals. This developed into a kind of romanticised cult of the *Ostjude*. The First World War helped to bring this about. As Stencl comments in his memoirs, the encounter between German Jewish soldiers fighting in Eastern Europe and the Jews of Poland and Russia and their culture was often revelatory for the former:

> The German-Jewish soldier did not return to his "homeland" from the First World War as bewildered and depressed as his "comrade" in battle, the German soldier. No matter how assimilated and Germanised he, the German Jew, may have been, in the occupied territories of Poland, Lithuania and the Ukraine he found his brothers, the Eastern European Jews. He had "discovered" the *Ostjuden.*[23]

These Eastern Jews seemed to embody a tradition which the westernised Jews had lost, as Gershom Scholem remarks in his autobiography:

> *In jedem Juden aus Russland, Polen, Galizien, der uns begegnete, sahen wir etwas wie eine Inkarnation des Baalschem und jedenfalls des unverstellten und uns faszinierenden jüdischen Wesens.*[24]

The nostalgic fascination which Scholem describes can be seen in various literary works which appeared in response to this new climate of interest: in Martin Buber's Hassidic stories; Alfred Döblin's *Reise in Polen* (Journey in Poland), 1926; Joseph Roth's *Juden auf Wanderschaft* (Wandering Jews), 1927; in the text and drawings of the book *Das ostjüdische Antlitz* (The face of the Eastern Jew) by Arnold Zweig and Hermann Struck; and in the work of Else Lasker-Schüler.

This climate of opinion was reflected in a growing interest in Yiddish literature. In 1920 Fritz Mordechai Kaufmann published a collection of Yiddish folksongs, and in the course of the twenties several important modern Yiddish literary works appeared in German translation, including H.D. Nomberg's short story *Fliglman*[25] and Dovid Bergelson's novel *Nokh alemen*[26] (When all's said and done). Various Yiddish poems and short stories appeared in the

German Jewish press, including, of course, those by Avrom Nokhem Stencl.

***

It is easy to visualise why this handsome, young, ingenuous Yiddish poet from a Hassidic, *shtetl* background seemed to embody the romanticised image of the "genuine" *Ostjude* in the eyes of the German-Jewish intelligentsia of Berlin. Else Lasker-Schüler, who invented romantic names for all her favourites, called him by the exotic Eastern-sounding name "Hamid" and mythologised him in her 1924 poem "Abraham Stenzel" as a child of nature, who also embodied the wisdom and holiness of the ancient Jewish heritage.[27]

Stencl was particularly fortunate in finding three enthusiastic devotees and translators of his work: Abraham Suhl, Elisabeth Wöhler and Etta Federn-Kohlhaas; thanks to them, many of Stencl's poems appeared in German translation in newspapers and journals,[28] often before they had been published in Yiddish. At least eleven volumes of poetry in Yiddish appeared in Germany between 1924 and 1936,[29] and two volumes in German translation: *Fischerdorf* (Fishing Village), 1931, and *Ring des Saturn,* (Ring of Saturn), 1932.[30] The original Yiddish version of the former did not appear till 1933, and the latter was, to my knowledge, never published in Yiddish. Some of the poems of *Fischerdorf* were read on the radio, and Stencl himself took part in poetry readings together with Jewish writers in both German and Yiddish. Stencl became celebrated in German Jewish literary circles, enjoying the approbation of well known contemporary figures such as the actor Ludwig Hardt, the writer Arnold Zweig, the critic Julius Bab, Alfred Richard Meyer, the president of the German Writers' Association and even Thomas Mann, who wrote to the latter praising *Fischerdorf*.

An article by Abraham Suhl, Stencl's first translator[31] illustrates most vividly the way in which the "cult" of the *Ostjude* helped to bring Stencl to prominence in Berlin Jewish society. The piece begins with a contrast between the Westernised Jews of Germany and the persona of this young poet:

> Are we still as young as this, we Jews? We are an ancient people, with ancient heads, heavy from too much thought! And now, see, here comes one of our ancient people, dancing about, supple, light as air, a cork bobbing on the waves, dances — a child, a shepherd, a faun... Oh, we Europeans wear seven layers of clothing, all buttoned up to the neck, with our stiff collars choking us. Full of pride, we do not know ourselves any more: do not know that we are naked under our clothing. But he is like a puppy dog, rolling in the snow, when God gives him snow, cavorting in the green grass in the springtime, and when he loves you he is humble and skips up to you... So, with doggy love in his heart, he went out into the world, into the huge city, trotted, a little dog, through its murderous chaos, slept in railway stations and stared with amazement, full of longing, at this strange world.

This is no objective critique of Stencl or his work, but rather an expression of Suhl's nostalgia for something which he had lost. While in his eyes the western Jew was old, tired, and his true identity was hidden, even from himself, under his "seven layers of clothing," the young Yiddish poet embodied a charming naiveté and spontaneity, closeness to nature, and an innocent loving heart.

According to Suhl, the western Jews had attempted in vain to compensate for lost authenticity by searching for it in other cultures, for example, through jazz. Suhl feels this was no longer necessary because Yiddish literature and figures like Stencl are proof that the genuine, original Jewish culture was, after all, still alive:

> Do we need negroes and jazz bands, in order to get back to nature? — The primeval melody, the original nakedness is still among us! Shepherds sing new songs, and they are the old psalms. David is still being born of our blood. And he plays and he dances... The miracles and the biblical stories never end. As long as poets shall live!

Other critics discussed Stencl's work itself in more detail, some pointed out the modernism in his poetry, but all the commentators emphasised the poet's closeness to nature and his ability to capture its essence. An article on the German edition of *Fischerdorf*, for example, finished with the words:

> Life in Nature is powerful and deep. The poet from the East has understood it in his own way and formed it in verses which are densely textured, objective and vivid, but above all else, filled with wonderful, painful awareness of the suffering of the living creature. A.N. Stencl is a poet, for his creative principle is: inwardness.[32]

The Poems

Stencl's large corpus of poetry encompasses many themes and demonstrates his mastery of a range of forms and styles: short lyrical verse, longer narrative poems, the sonnet and the ballad. Underlying his oeuvre from the German period is the existential struggle between his previous identity in Poland in the religious world of his father and his new life as a modern poet in a secular society, which engendered feelings of guilt and betrayal, but also of freedom and renewal. The poems reflect the polarities of countryside and city, the contrast between Stencl's empathy with the natural world and his ambivalent reactions to the chaos of the modern metropolis — a theme which places him very clearly within the sphere of German Expressionist writing of the early twentieth century. The poems in *All My Young Years* are selected from two of the books of his Weimar period: *Un du bist Got* (And you are God), published in 1925, and the later *Fisherdorf* (1933). These two very different works reveal Stencl's poetic development and the scope of his creativity during his German period. They focus on several of the key themes arising from his experiences of that time, which remain central in his work.

Un du bist Got is Stencl's second published collection of poetry, and here the young poet wrestled with the anguish and inner conflicts of these early years. He characterised the genesis of these poems as a "struggle with Satan... with my own shadow! I was searching for the *ikh* and trying to find the *du* and to save myself from both of them… each poem was an attempt to find a hold, to save myself, to walk a tightrope... getting the taste of life on my outstretched tongue..."[33] The poet describes receiving a letter from his father enquiring about his son's publication:

> Letters from home always drove me mad!... When I had read one of these letters, I sat for hours in a distracted state — I realised there was a world where hearts are bound to each other with a thousand threads and however much you pull yourself away from them, they only become more and more tightly fastened — you wriggle as if in a net and sink in an eternal chasm of love and of hatred for yourself... In the letter my father enquired about the book: he had read about a book by me in a review in a Warsaw newspaper. He had understood some of the lines which were quoted, but not others. And why had I not sent him the book? And above all, what is the meaning of the title of the book?
>
> Can I write to him, that this is a last, agonising, bloody tearing myself away from what was — from my whole being? — that [...] my whole *ikh* is undergoing a change — has to change! And even the *du* [...] has no permanence — hardly any feeling... it means creation, shaping, reflecting itself in a human being [...] seeking one's reflection in a running stream?... As if one person were pursuing another, to become one—[34]

The breathless, fragmented style of Stencl's self-questioning here conveys the intensity of the conflict within him, relived here nearly fifty years later; this same anguish finds expression in the themes, images and forms of the poems of *Un du bist Got*.

The book consists of sixty poems arranged in three sections. The first section, entitled *Un du bist Got*[35] is a dialogue between the poet and the elusive "*du*", the God that he is seeking. The poems express his longing for union with the divine Other, but also acute awareness of his alienation from it. In the second section *Un ale meynen, az zey lebn* (And they all think they are alive),[36] the quest opens out into a consideration of the poet's relationship with the world and other people: the conflict between the longing to be part of the world and the desire for creative seclusion. The final section, with the Hebrew title *Ve'eheye ketsipor boded al gag* (And I shall be like a lonely bird on the roof),[37] also focuses on the poet's isolation in the world, particularly in the city, but here Stencl moves from the narrow confines of the individual self, affirming the poet's mission to speak to all humankind.

The poems, almost all in blank verse, have strong affinity with German and Yiddish Expressionist poetry, in their themes of the city and the agony of human beings, their exclamatory style and their vivid, often violent imagery. There are also clear elements of the Romantic tradition. The speaker who wanders through these poems is essentially the self-conscious "I" of Romantic poetry, seeking individual fulfilment, depicted in a variety of images which combine pathos and self-irony: the dying swan, the helpless sailor trying to survive a storm in a boat with torn sails and useless oars, or the miller crying out for water as the well bubbles up beside his feet. The other significant particularity of this poetry lies in its rich store of imagery and expression drawn from Jewish religious language and ritual. Such a fusion of European literary and Jewish religious traits gives much modern Yiddish poetry its specific dynamic, and here it emphasises the tension which Stencl feels between the two worlds in which his self resides.

It is not difficult to see why Stencl did not send his father a copy of this book. The gulf between the ordered, God-centred universe of Stencl's parents' generation and the way in which the concept of God and the religious imagery is used in the poet's existential quest is completely unbridgeable. Stencl deliberately flouts tradition and taboos in his conceptualisation of God. In the powerful poem *Iz dokh Got ful in ale gasn* (Still All the Streets are God-filled) the omnipresence of God is accompanied by violent imagery of mutilation. In other poems, where a sense of union with God is achieved, it is only through the annihilation of the self:

Un du shoymst in mayne beyner,
Vayser vayn in vayse bekhers —

Got, Got,
Gebundene shvakhkeyt in mir
Mit oysgeshtrektn vaysn haldz...
Mit oysgeshtrekte vayse glider...

And you foam in my bones,
White wine in white goblets —

God, God,
Trussed-up weakness inside me
With an outstretched white neck ...
With outstretched white limbs ...

Here the colour white has both positive and negative symbolic resonance: the *ikh* drinks the essence of God like white wine, which enters his very bones — an image of purification and fusion with the divine. At the same time, white seems to denote death, as it traditionally does in Judaism, in the whiteness of his stretched-out neck and limbs.

Stencl departs most radically from religious tradition in his arrogation of the imagery of the Bible and of Hassidic worship in a secular and individualistic context which would be seen by observant Jews as blasphemous, as in the poem *Nisht vagn zol keyner...* (No-One Should Dare):

Nisht vagn zol keyner
In mayn kodshey-kodoshim tsu kumen,
Vu shotns shvarts bataleste
Tuen shtile avoydes
Koyrim falndik un shorkhndik.

No-one should dare
Come into my Holy of Holies,
Where black prayer-shawled shadows
Do silent service
Falling on their knees and rustling.

Here and throughout the poem, the language of worship is applied to the self: the shrine is within the *ikh*. Within that sacred place — his poetic inner life — the worshippers in prayer shawls are prostrating themselves before the Holy of Holies which is the self. In this way Stencl uses the imagery of his old tradition to struggle towards a new definition of the holy: the realm of poetry and the humanistic view of the world.

Despite the prevailing anguish and often despair in the poems, the first two sections end on a positive note of reconciliation, in which the Hassidic background of the poet plays a major role. The first finishes with the *ikh* achieving the longed-for union with the divine through an ecstatic Hassidic dance, while the second section ends with a mysterious allegory *Dos shlisele* (The Little Key). In its strange, dream-like atmosphere and esoteric symbolism this vision seems inspired by the tales of Hassidic rebbes, especially the mystical stories of Reb Nachman Bratslaver. This mysterious tale seems to represent the rejection of aesthetic solipsism in favour of commitment to humankind, through which the profane can be purified and transfigured into the good and beautiful.

The final poem of the whole collection, *Ale mayne yunge yorn* (All My Young Years), is ambiguous. It can be interpreted as affirming this commitment to humanity. The poet contemplates his past and his future, visualising his past years as milestones lying on the path which leads to God. Though he sees the future years as *balodnt mit shvere shteyner* (weighed with heavy stones), the final image can be interpreted as a positive resolution, suggesting that his heart remains alive through human contact, and that through the poet, others find their way to God:

In mitn veg
Unter mayn letstn vaysn shteyn
Vet eybik tsaplen mayn harts
Far yedn farbaygeyer
Vos geyt tsu dir.

In the middle of the road
Under my final white stone
My heart will quiver always
With every passer-by
Who journeys toward you.

These last lines can however also be read as a vision of deep pessimism: while others find their way to God, the *ikh* remains inert on the roadside, never achieving union with the God whom he has been seeking throughout these poems. The ambiguity at the end of the book reflects the unresolved inner conflict of *Un du bist Got*.[38]

***

Fisherdorf forms an extraordinary contrast to *Un du bist Got*. The poems were written in 1926, after Stencl had spent some time in the village of Neuendorf on the peninsula of Wolin. In his memoirs he describes the joy he felt at resolving the conflicts of the earlier poems and finding himself:

> It is worth all the spectres, and all the seven kinds of hell to feel suddenly that a canvas has emerged from the cobwebs and is spread out before you, stretching from the depths of hell to the seventh heaven. You climb up it from stage to stage, and from all the constellations of images, living beings emerge [...] You stand face to face with your *du* as in a bright mirror [...] You mould your own self out of pieces of earth and you capture your own life. At that time I called these poems 'still-lifes'.[39]

This description is apposite, for the poems are like paintings. The harmony the poet felt allowed him to turn from the turmoil of the self and focus entirely on the outside world: the *ikh* seldom appears. Jewish themes are completely absent, and the poems observe the lives of the peasants and the fishing community in a rural German village, and their two spheres of work — the land and the sea. Stencl shows deep understanding of these people, of the often menacing power of nature, and the complex interdependence between it and the farmers and fishermen. The land and sea become like living beings in the poems.

Like Impressionist paintings, the poems capture and eternalise fleeting moments and incidents in people's lives. Stencl depicts without sentimentality the dignity of the toil-worn human being. In *Nokh der arbet* (After Work), he describes the peasants and their animals resting after a day's labour. The slow and stately rhythm adds dignity to the theme:

Oyfn shvel fun der vayser khate
Roykhert s'poyerl zayn letste fayke
Un varft arayn a getseylt vort.
Un zayn opgearbet ferdl in shtal
Zupt groyse zupn
Un kratst mit a vakldiker podkeve.

S'brekht azoy mikhayedik in di beyner
Azoy menukhedik gut,
Un dem hunts oyfgeshtelte oyern
Khapn oyf shtiklekh shmuesn
Mekoyekhn morgndikn veter...

On the doorstep of the white hut
The old farmer smokes a last pipe
And throws in his measured word.
And the weary horse in the stable
Mouths up big sips of water
And scratches with a shaky shoe.

Something burns so joyfully,
So peacefully in those bones,
And the dog's pricked-up ears
Catch little snatches of talk
About tomorrow's weather...

Stencl's attention to little details like the dog pricking up its ears to hear the fragments of conversation brings the scene to life. Often the essence of a human being or animal is captured by such small characteristic gestures, as in the moment when one horse lays its head gently on the neck of the other, in *Oyf der lonke* (In the Meadows), or in *Hoyf mit botshan* (Farmyard with Stork), with its fluttering doves, laden carts, melancholy horse walking round and round pulling the creaking threshing machine, and the unexpected, humorously and affectionately observed stork on the roof:

Blaybt er shteyn, der groyser botshan
Oyf zayn oysgebetn shtroydakh,
Hoybt oyf a langn, darn fus
Tsu zayn nideriker rie
Un trakht tsu a harblekhn inyen.

The big stork stays standing
On its roof of padded straw
And, lifting a long, thin leg
To its myopic eye,
Reflects on a difficult matter.

Stencl's depictions of old people are particularly striking. He does not beautify or sentimentalise them but often uses startling, grotesque imagery to bring out the more painful ravages of old age and hardship. There is the old fisherman with his bones rattling "like empty bottles lining a tiny sack" or the vivid but disturbing description of the old bilberry seller, *Di balade fun der borevke-bobe* (The Ballad of the Bilberry Seller). The first lines of this poem focus on the hands of the old woman, comparing them with bushes torn out by the roots:

Aroysgerisene kushakes mit vortslen
Zeyen oys ire oysgetriknte hent.
Un di borevkes vos zi mest on
Zaynen zikher di aroysgerinene blut-tropn.

Like shrubs with torn-out roots:
Her dried-up hands resemble this.
And the bilberries that she's weighing
Are surely drops of dripping blood.

Here the image of the dry roots is dominant, so that the old woman's hands have a disembodied, dehumanised quality. Stencl's image is violent: the torn out shrubs/ hands are bleeding, the bilberries — her livelihood — being the drops of blood. Inanimate nature is made into a metaphor of human suffering.

The perspective changes in the second two stanzas, as the omniscient author intervenes to tell the story of the old woman's life:

Ven zi iz a yung blut geven,
Hot zi shoyn ire ershte milkh farkoyft in shtot,
Yener, vos hot ir dem boykh gemakht,
Hot zi ahingefirt vi a fule milkh-kan!

When she was still a blood-young girl
She'd already sold her first milk in town,
The one who had made her belly big
Led her there full as a frothing churn!

The first impression is that she had sold dairy produce, until the second two lines shatter this illusion, with the revelation that she herself was the "frothing churn", exploited (as a wet-nurse?) by the man who had made her pregnant. The representation of the woman as an inanimate object reinforces the idea of dehumanisation which was implicit in the first stanza. The final lines develop this imagery further: the sunken cheeks of the old woman make of her simply "a tin milk-churn, a dented bent one."

Stencl's characteristic technique of placing the metaphor in the foreground is very effective in creating this powerful image of a toilworn old woman. His sensitive, but direct and unsentimental treatment of the fate of the poor is evident in many other poems of this collection and is also characteristic of Stencl's later London poetry.

The underlying motif of the whole cycle is nature, or rather the relationship between nature and the human being, which can be a partnership or a fight for survival. This dual aspect is particularly evident in the sea-poems, of which a striking example is *Shturem-lid* (Storm-Song) with its dramatic imagery and tone reminiscent of the sea-robber poems of the early Brecht.

All in all, *Fisherdorf* is one of Stencl's most impressive poetic creations. His ability to evoke a milieu and a culture which was so different from his own, his depiction of the complex relationship between human being and nature, and of the dignity of work, as well as the technical virtuosity of the poems — the vivid, often grotesque imagery, the monumental quality of these "still-lifes", the subtle flow of the rhythms — all these qualities reveal a mature and technically accomplished poet.

Stencl went on to publish several further collections of poetry before he left Germany in November 1936, of which the most impressive are perhaps the 1934 sonnet-cycle on the death of his father, *Fundervaytns* (From afar), and the extensive series of poems on Biblical themes, *Mazl tole* (The Sign of the Ram, 1935). In the latter theme he was probably influenced by Else Lasker-Schüler's *Hebräische Balladen* (Hebrew Ballads) which had appeared in 1913, but his approach to the Biblical material is very different from hers.[40]

Stencl in Whitechapel

The transition from Berlin, where he was quite a celebrity in a vibrant literary milieu, to anonymity in the East End of London cannot have been easy for Stencl. He does not seem to have written specifically about this, but several powerful and disturbing poems from the early forties addressed to Elisabeth Wöhler testify to the emotional agony and guilt which he had to work through, in the light of the gradually emerging knowledge about the horrors of the Holocaust.

Politically Stencl was uncompromisingly socialist; like most of the London Yiddish-speaking intellectuals his faith in the Soviet Union remained undiminished for many years, and in the war years he wrote a series of ecstatic poems in praise of Stalin and the Red Army. It was not until the truth of the persecution and execution of Jewish writers in the early fifties became irrefutable that disillusionment with the great revolutionary dream set in. He never betrayed his socialist beliefs, however, and a constant theme in his poetry remains his deep concern for social justice for the poor and dispossessed.

From the beginning he was devoted to the Jewish district of Whitechapel, which he called his *shtetl d'Britn.*[41] Most of the immigrants, refugees from poverty and pogroms in Eastern Europe, had arrived in this area from the 1880s onwards, and Yiddish remained the main language there until well into the nineteen-forties when its slow decline began, as the children of the first and second immigrant generations became increasingly anglicised and left the East End for the middle-class suburbs. Stencl began publishing books of poetry from shortly after his arrival,[42] and from 1940 on he started publishing pamphlets in Yiddish which developed into his Yiddish journal *Loshn un lebn*. It contained not only his own memoirs, essays and poems, but also the work of many other Yiddish writers from London and elsewhere, together with translations from other languages. Dovid Katz, who knew Stencl very well, records his pain at watching Stencl "hawking the journal by himself on streets and streetcorners [...] When he spotted a Jew on the street, he would approach him and in an almost beggarly tone, say *Koyfts a heft* (buy an issue)."[43]

Stencl's lasting achievement was the foundation of the institution *Fraynd fun yidish loshn* (Friends of the Yiddish language) and its literary Saturday afternoon meetings. In its heyday up to two hundred people would attend to hear and participate in talks and readings from Yiddish literature. The literary *Shabes-nokhmitik* continues to this day in Toynbee Hall, in Stencl's Whitechapel.

Stencl's London poetry focuses mainly on the theme of Whitechapel, which he represents as the heir of the great centres of Jewish culture in Eastern Europe. He immortalises the poor Jews of the East End, painting striking portraits of many of the well known local characters of the time. His London work is undeniably very uneven in quality: he simply published too much, without taking the time to edit and revise sufficiently. Where he did use his undoubted editorial skills, some of his work certainly stands comparison with the best of his Berlin poetry.[44]

Until the end of his life he dedicated all his energies to his passionate campaign for the survival of Yiddish culture. Gradually, however, he realised that his beloved Yiddish language probably had very little future as a living mass medium, and his later writings in *Loshn un lebn* become ever more pessimistic. Though he was, as Dovid Katz puts it, one of those figures who "in their lifetime were treated by their followers as 'gurus', charismatic-mystical figures with the power to bewitch",[45] there is no denying the fact that these followers were a relatively small band in a society where Yiddish was not a major cultural focus.

Stencl has never been accorded the critical attention which the best of his work certainly deserves. He has been systematically ignored or even reviled by the Yiddish academic establishment, as Dovid Katz and Jeffrey Grossman have demonstrated.[46] The time is ripe for a reassessment of his literary achievement and of his role in Yiddish culture in Berlin and London during two pivotal periods. The funeral oration has not yet been made over Yiddish in London, which is now enjoying quite a significant academic and popular cultural revival. Stencl's work may eventually bear fruit in ways that he could not have foreseen, and it is our hope that this selection of his poetry may play a role in furthering the reawakened interest in Yiddish culture, and in bringing to an unjustly neglected poet the attention he merits.

Heather Valencia

Footnotes

[1] Hassidism was a movement which arose in eighteenth century Poland. The adherents grouped themselves round various inspirational religious leaders, or *rebbes*. Early Hassidim rejected the orthodox tradition in favour of an individual approach to God through music, dancing and prayer, where devotees strove to reach a state of mystical ecstasy.

[2] Educated men also conducted their correspondence in Hebrew. The letters to Stencl from his father are in Hebrew, usually with a short note in Yiddish from his mother. (Stencl archive, School of Oriental and African Studies, University of London)

[3] See Stencl's literary journal *Loshn un lebn* (Language and Life), December 1964, p. 21 ff. Stencl published his memoirs of the Berlin years in this journal between 1967 and 1974. The institutionalised anti-semitism in the Polish army and the impossibility of keeping to the Jewish laws and rituals led many religious families to go to any lengths to avoid military service.

[4] His poem-cycle *Fisherdorf* (Fishing Village) was set in this rural and fishing community which is now in Poland.

[5] For a discussion of Stencl's relationship with Elisabeth Wöhler, see below, p. 10 ff.

[6] *Loshn un lebn,* Nov/Dec. 1974, pp. 26-27.

[7] The Hebrew and Yiddish words for "pomegranate".

[8] Mainly on account of his poem "Uri-Tsvi farn tseylem", (Uri-Zvi before the Cross) which was printed in the shape of the cross on which Jesus was crucified.

[9] Walter Laqueur, *Weimar, a Cultural History, 1918-1933,* New York: Perigee Books, 1980, pp. 227-228.

[10] *Loshn un lebn*, Oct/Nov. 1968, p. 24. In this introduction, all prose translations are mine. All quoted translations from Stencl's poetry are taken from the present book.

[11] 2. Samuel, 20:19. Daniel Charney, *Di velt iz kaylekhdik* (The world is round), Tel-Aviv, 1963, p.35.

[12] For a more detailed discussion of the relationship between the two poets, see Heather Valencia, *Else Lasker-Schüler und Abraham Nochem Stenzel. Eine unbekannte Freundschaft,* Frankfurt am Main/New York: Campus Verlag, 1995.

[13] See p. 38.

[14] The correspondence from Stencl's father and from Elisabeth Wöhler is in the Stencl archive in the School of Oriental and African Studies, University of London, and the letters and postcards from Else Lasker-Schüler are in the Lasker-Schüler archive in the Hebrew University, Jerusalem. The Elisabeth Wöhler archive at the Archiv Bibliographia Judaica, Frankfurt am Main contains all the materials relating to Stencl which Elisabeth Wöhler collected.

[15] Unpublished autobiographical sketch, Elizabeth Wöhler archive, Archiv Bibliographia Judaica, Frankfurt am Main.

[16] *Loshn un lebn*, Jan. 1967, p. 21.

[17] *Loshn un lebn*, Feb/March 1973, p. 23.

[18] *Loshn un lebn* February/April 1970, p. 23.

[19] Letter from Annette Neumann to A.N. Stencl, 19.7.1975, Stencl archive, School of Oriental and African Studies, University of London.

[20] The judge when sentencing Stencl to three months in Moabit Prison spoke scathingly of foreigners who purport to be artists but in reality are "promoting Bolshevik propaganda". *Der Moment*, 14 June 1925.

[21] Peter Gay, *Freud, Jews and other Germans*, New York: Oxford U.P., 1978, p. 110.

[22] *Loshn un lebn,* January 1968, p. 21.

[23] *Loshn un lebn*, Feb/March 1967, p. 35.

[24] "In every Jew from Russia, Poland or Galicia whom we met, we saw something like an incarnation of the Baalshem [the founder of Hassidism] or at least of the genuine essence of the Jewish soul, which fascinated us." Gershom Scholem, *Von Berlin nach Jerusalem*, (From Berlin to Jerusalem), Frankfurt am Main: Suhrkamp, 1977, p. 60.

[25] H.D. Nomberg, *Fliglman und andere Erzählungen und Bilder* [Fliglman and other stories and pictures], translated by Abraham Suhl, Leipzig, 1924.

[26] In German *Das Ende vom Lied* (The end of the story), translated by Alexander Eliasberg, Berlin, 1923.

[27] See p. 38.

[28] Among the publications in which these translations appeared were the *Jüdisches Wochenblatt*, Leipzig, the *Leipziger*

Jüdische Zeitung, the *Deutsch-Jüdische Volkszeitung* and the famous *Weltbühne*.

[29] According to Stencl, the German translation of *Fisherdorf* was among the works destroyed in the book-burning of 1933, but his books of poetry in Yiddish continued to be published until he left Germany in 1936. It is interesting that small Yiddish presses managed to print the works of Jewish writers under the noses of the Nazis, long after the official banning of "decadent" literature.

[30] *Fischerdorf,* translated by Etta Federn-Kohlhaas, Berlin-Wilmersdorf: Kartell Lyrischer Autoren, 1931, and *Ring des Saturn*, translated by Elisabeth Wöhler, Berlin: Rabenpresse, 1932.

[31] Abraham Suhl, "A.N. Stenzel", *Leipziger Jüdische Zeitung*, 10 February 1924.

[32] o.p., "Hinweis auf einen Dichter. Der Lyriker A.N. Stenzel." (Introducing a poet: the lyricist A.N. Stencl) in: *Prager Presse*, 25.5.1931.

[33] *Loshn un lebn*, July/August 1971, p. 24.

[34] *Loshn un lebn,* March/April 1971, pp. 19-20 (Two numbers of the journal bear the date "March/April 1971". This is the second one, which should actually be dated "May/June".)

[35] The first seven poems of this selection (pp. 42-55) belong to section one of the book.

[36] pp. 56-71.

[37] pp. 72-81.

[38] These first anguished struggles to affirm the value of a humanistic philosophy reach a harmonious resolution ten years later, at the end of a cycle of sonnets on the death of his father, when Stencl is able confidently to set his father's philosophy and his own side by side, equally worthy of honour: "God was there when you stood before Him/ He trembled in your blood./ And now, when my heart is full of faith/the human stands before the human.//[...] Just as you, father, stood before God/So I will stand before every human being." (*Fundervaytns* [From afar], p. 22.)

[39] *Losh un lebn,* July/August 1971, p. 26.

[40] For a discussion of these poems and of the influence of Else Lasker-Schüler on Stencl, see Valencia, *Else Lasker-Schüler und Abraham Nochem Stenzel.*

[41] ie “British shtetl”. He also called Whitechapel “Yerusholayim d’Britn” (the Jerusalem of Britain). Both names are a reference to the well-known phrase “Yerusholayim d’Lite” (the Jerusalem of Lithuania), by which Yiddish-speaking Jews referred to Vilna (Vilnius), the famous centre of Jewish culture.

[42] All the work from Stencl’s London period was published by the Yiddish printer and publisher Narod Press. The father of the owners, Israel Naroditsky (1874-1942) stipulated in his will that all Stencl’s books and journals were to be published by his sons until Stencl’s death. (see Dovid Katz, “Stencl of Whitechapel”, *The Mendele Review*, vol. 7, no. 3, 30 March 2003. http://www2.trincoll.edu/~mendele/tmrarc.htm) See also *Jewish Books in Whitechapel,* ed. Marion Aptroot, London: Duckworth, 1991.

[43] Katz, “Stencl of Whitechapel”.

[44] See S.S. Prawer, *A.N. Stencl, Poet of Whitechapel*, Oxford: Oxford Centre for Postgraduate Hebrew Studies, 1984.

[45] Katz, “Stencl of Whitechapel”.

[46] cf. Katz, op. cit., and Jeffrey Grossman, “Farvos ignorirn di literatur-historiker A.N. Shtentslen?” (Why do the literary historians ignore A.N. Stencl?), in: *Oksforder yidish, A Yearbook of Yiddish Studies*. Vol. 1, ed. Dovid Katz, London: Harwood Academic Publishers, 1990, pp. 91-106.

Stencl and Else Lasker-Schüler

Stencl met the poet Else Lasker-Schüler in the Romanische Café in August 1922. She was twenty-eight years older than he was, but a deep friendship developed between them. The older poet had many emotional attachments, often to younger men; her relationship with Stencl was coloured by her fascination, revealed in her writings, with the world of Eastern European Jewry and with the mystical tradition of Hassidism. To her Stencl appeared to embody much of this authentic Jewish tradition for which she, like many of the German-Jewish intellectuals, felt a strong romantic yearning.

Stencl wrote very sensitively about his relationship with Lasker-Schüler in his memoirs in *Loshn un lebn* between 1968 and 1973.[1] Two poems about her from his Berlin period are extant, the first written immediately after their first meeting. The Yiddish version of this seven-part poem appears to be lost, but a typescript of Abraham Suhl's German translation, entitled *Meiner älteren Schwester Einfalt* (To my older Sister, Simplicity) is in the Archiv Bibliographia Judaica in Frankfurt.[2] One part of this German version was published in *Die Weltbühne* in 1926.[3]

The other poem, entitled *Elze Lasker-Shiler* was written in 1927, after the burial of Lasker-Schüler's son Paul. It is in two sections, and was translated into German by Elisabeth Wöhler.[4] Only the first section is extant in the Yiddish original, in Stencl's manuscript in the Archiv Bibliographia Judaica.

Else Lasker-Schüler wrote one poem about Stencl, of which two versions in manuscript form are extant in the Else Lasker-Schüler Archive in Jerusalem. The shorter of the two was published by Margarete Kupper in *Literaturwissenschaftliches Jahrbuch der Görries Gesellschaft*, vol. 8, 1967, p.178. The longer version published here, which bears the date 1.7.1924, also exists as a copy in Elisabeth

Wöhler's handwriting in the Archiv Bibliographia Judaica, Frankfurt am Main. In my opinion it is the later and better version of the poem.

After Else Lasker-Schüler left Germany for Palestine in 1933, she continued to be very concerned about Stencl, and made efforts to help him escape to Palestine. She sent him and Elisabeth Wöhler a series of postcards, some of which contain coded references to his plight.[5] Stencl's memoirs, the postcards, and the two poems printed below give insights into this unusual and significant friendship.

Heather Valencia

Footnotes

[1] These extracts appear in German translation in Valencia, *Else Lasker-Schüler und Abraham Nochem Stenzel.*

[2] See also Valencia, op. cit., pp. 116-19.

[3] *Die Weltbühne*, No. 6, 9.2.1926.

[4] Wöhler's translation was published in various publications. See also Valencia, op. cit., pp. 120-21.

[5] See Valencia, op. cit., pp. 125-130.

A.N. Stencl, courtesy of S.S. Prawer

Abraham Stenzel

by Else Lasker-Schüler

Als Abraham ganz jung war,
Nannte ihn Gott: Hamid.

Ich weiß es noch, denn erst viertausend
Und ein Schaltjahr ist es her.

Ich hing zwar noch am Baum
Im Schatten einer Cocospalme.

Mein Spielgefährte, Abraham Stenzel,
Gärte mit dem Mark im Stamm.

Begraben sind die Bibeljahre längst -
Wir beide tragen nur noch sehnsüchtig den Flor

Um unsern blauen Hut,
Der demütig die Stirn vor Gott bedeckt.

Der Hamid ist der Dichter des Jargons,
Des Ghettoplatts.

Wenn er es spricht, hilflos und rührend,
Pocht an mein Herz das Jugendvolkslied.

Er ist ein inniger innerlicher Dichter
Und seine Unverfälschtheit macht ihn liebenswert.

Wenn wir nach Mitternacht
Im Winter vom Romanischen Caféhaus

Zusammen leiernd durch den Schnee
Wie durch die Wüste trabten,

Kopf geneigt — überall Sahara:
Zwei edle Wüstentiere er und ich.

In seinen grünen Jordanaugen
Erinnern Träume sich vom Erzvater?

Und jedem Südenwinde blickt er nach,
Der über seine schwarzen Haare streicht.

Ich liebe seiner schönen Verse Kabala
Sie trägt sein frommes Angesicht als Medaillon.

Abraham Stenzel

by Else Lasker-Schüler
Translated by Heather Valencia

When Abraham was very young,
Got called him: Hamid.

I remember this, for it's only
Four thousand years and one leap year ago.

I still hung in the trees
Shaded by a coconut palm.

My playmate Abraham Stenzel
Bubbled up with the sap of the tree.

The bible years are buried long ago —
Yearning, we both still wear a mourning band

Round our blue hat, which modestly
Covers our forehead before God.

Hamid is the poet of Yiddish,
The patois of the ghetto.

When he speaks it, touchingly helpless,
The folksong of my youth knocks at my heart.

He is a fervent, soulful poet
Lovable in his uncorruptedness.

When after midnight, in the winter,
Swaying together through the snow

From the Romanische Café
We tramped, as through the desert,

Heads bent — all around Sahara,
Two noble desert beasts, the two of us.

In his green Jordan-eyes
Do dreams remember the Father?

He gazes after every southern wind
Which ruffles his black hair.

I love the Kabbala of his lovely verse.
It bears his pious countenance as an amulet.

עלזע לאַסקער-שילער

איך וועל דיר אויסטעשן צוויי וויגן-טרעטער,
זיי צונאָגלען צוביידע זײַטן ערד.
דו וועסט זיצן צוקאָפּנס
און אײַנוויגן דאָס געוויין פֿון די וועלט :
„אויף אונדזער זײַט ערד
איז אַלץ פֿאַרקערט,
איז אַלץ פֿאַרקערט,
און אַ מאַמע-האַרץ איז בלינד,
וויגעלע, ציגעלע, מײַן קינד.“

Else Lasker-Schüler by A.N. Stencl

I will carve you two cradle-rockers,
And nail them to both sides of the earth.
You will sit at its head,
and rock the weeping world to sleep :
"On our side of the earth,
All is topsy-turvy,
All is topsy-turvy,
and a mother's heart is blind,
Rock-a-bye, hush-a-bye, my child."

Translated by Heather Valencia

פֿון: א.נ. שטענצל, און דו ביסט גאָט
(לײַפּציג: שמש, 1925)

אויף אַלע פֿיר אויסגעצויגן ...

אויף אַלע פֿיר אויסגעצויגן
ליגט מײַן כאָרכלענדיקע שוואַכקייט אין מיר,
אַ געבונדענע
און שרײַט:
– גאָט, גאָט

און דו שוימסט אין מײַנע ביינער,
ווײַסער ווײַן אין ווײַסע בעכערס – –

גאָט, גאָט,
געבונדענע שוואַכקייט אין מיר
מיט אויסגעשטרעקטן ווײַסן האַלדז ...
מיט אויסגעשטרעקטע ווײַסע גלידער ...

From:
Un du bist Got ("And You Are God")

Stretched Out On All Fours ...

Stretched out on all fours
My weakness wheezes within me,
Trussed-up inside,
And screams:
God, God —

And you foam in my bones,
White wine in white goblets — —

God, God,
Trussed-up weakness inside me
With an outstretched white neck ...
With outstretched white limbs ...

שיק איך מײַן תּפֿילה צו בלויען הימל ...

שיק איך מײַן תּפֿילה צו בלויען הימל
צו ריינעם הימל :
דו, וואָס האָסט אַזוי פֿיל בלוי,
דו, וואָס האָסט אַזוי פֿיל ריין,
אַלמאַכטיקער !
וואָס פֿאַר איין אָטעם דײַנעם
איז דער גאַנצער גרוי גאָר נישט געוואָרן
צו גאָר נישט,
און ווי קיינמאָל גאָר נישט געווען –
שענק אַ טראָפּן בלוי מיר,
שענק אַ נ'עוקץ ריין מיר,
אַלמאַכטיקער
לאָז מיך אין אָטעם דײַנעם –
נעפּל צערינען,
קיינמאָל, קיינמאָל גאָר נישט
און קיינמאָל גאָר נישט געווען ...

I Send My Prayer ...*

I send my prayer to the blue heaven,
To the pure sky:
You, who have so much of blue,
You, who have so much of pure,
Almighty One!
Through one breath of Yours
The whole grey is turned
To nothing, nothing
As if it never had been anything at all —
Give to me a drop of blue,
Give to me a dash of pure,
Almighty One,
Let me dissolve as mist
Inside your breath —
Never anything at all and never
Having been anything either ...

*Though untitled in the original publication, the contents page there lists it as "Merts-psalm" (March Psalm)

אין ווײַסן שוואַנען-לאַנד ...

אין ווײַסן שוואַנען-לאַנד,
מיט אַן אויסגעגלאָצטן שוואַנען-האַלדז,
פֿלי איך, מײַן לעצטן
„ברכו את אדוני ! ...“
אויסבלעזלען –
לאָזן ציטערדיקע רעדלעך
אַ רגע נאָך מיר ...

אין ווײַסן שוואַנען-לאַנד
וועט שטאַרבן מײַן לעצטע תּפֿילה,
מײַן ערשטע תּפֿילה מיט מיר –
צעבלעזלט אין מײַן מאַרך,
אין מײַנע בלוטן צערעדלט;
אין יעטוועדן טראָפּן באַזונדער !

אין ווײַסן שוואַנען-לאַנד
וועט בלײַבן מײַן תּפֿילה אַ הענגעדיקע –
ווײַסער הויך
אויף ווײַסע הימלען ...

In The White Swan-Land ...

In the white swan-land
With outstretched swan-neck
I fly, my last
"Blessed be God! ..."
Bubbling out of me —
Leaving trembling ripple-circles
For a few moments in my wake ...

In the white swan-land
My last prayer will die,
My first prayer die with me —
Dissolved as bubbles in my marrow,
Rippled as small circles in my blood —
In each drop separately!

In the white swan-land
My prayer will hover in the air —
White breath
In white skies ...

ווּ אַנקערן ? ...

ווּ אַנקערן ?
אַז כ'האָב מורא פֿאַר פֿעלדזן,
אַז כ'האָב מורא פֿאַר וועלן,
און מײַן זעגל איז געלעכערט – –

צווײ שוואַרץ פֿאַרלאָשענע טהרה-ליכט,
שטעקן מײַנע רודערס
אין שוואַרץ צעווילדעוועטן וועלן-געווירבל,
און מײַן שיפֿל וואַקלט און וואַקלט.

ווּ, ווּ ?
אַז כ'בין אײנער, אײנער,
פֿון שוואַרץ צעפּאַטלטע ים-אינד אַ געיאָגטער,
פֿון ווילד צעשוימטע ים-אינד אַ געהעצטער,

ווּ, ווּ ?
אַז נאָר פֿינסטערניש און פֿינסטערניש,
אַז נאָר פֿינסטערניש און פֿינסטערניש !

ווּ, ווּ ?
אַז – –
אַז – –

Where to Anchor? ...

Where to anchor?
Since I'm afraid of rocks,
Since I'm afraid of waves
And my sail is full of holes — —

And my oars become stuck —
Two black-extinguished corpse lights —
In the black raging turmoil of waves
And my little boat shaking, shaking.

Where, where?
Since I am here alone
And I'm hunted by black dishevelled waves
And I'm rushed at by wild-foaming waves.

Where, where?
Since there is only darkness and darkness,
Since there is only darkness and darkness!

Where, where?
Since — —
Because — —

איז דאָך גאָט פֿול אין אַלע גאַסן ...

איז דאָך גאָט פֿול אין אַלע גאַסן,
און ווען ער איז נישטאָ –
טראָגן מיר אים דאָך
ביז שפּיצן פֿינגער.

קום,
וועלן מיר שפּאַלטן פֿלייש אין פֿלייש,
וועלן מיר שפּאַלטן הימלען אין הימלען – –
– – – – – – – – – – – – – – –

איז דאָך גאָט פֿול אין אַלע גאַסן !

קום,
ברעכן מיר אָרעמס אויף,
ביז די הערצער אויפֿברעכן ! –
און זיך פֿאַלן אין די הערצער !

האַקן פֿון הערצער,
פֿלעכטן פֿון הערצער
איינעם,
איינעם !

איז דאָך גאָט פֿול אין אַלע גאַסן – –

Still All the Streets Are God-filled ...

Still all the streets are God-filled.
And if He is not there —
We will still carry Him
Right to the quick of our fingers.

Come,
We will split flesh in flesh,
We will split heavens in heavens — —
— — — — — — — — — — —

Still all the streets are God-filled!

Come,
We will break arms open,
Until hearts break open! —
And fall into each other's hearts!

Hack-out from hearts,
Braid together from hearts
One,
One!

Still all the streets are God-filled — —

האָט אַ דונער אין בוים געטראָפֿן ...

האָט אַ דונער אין בוים געטראָפֿן,

מײַן נשמה איז אַ צווײַגעלע,
אויפֿן צווײַגעלע איז אַ גאָלדן פֿייגעלע געשטאַנען.

מישן זיך זייערע בלוטן – –

ווו וועט דער ווינט אַ פֿלייט געפֿינען ?

ווער וועט פֿאַר אויפֿגייענדיקע זון
אַ מאָרגן-ליד טשוויטשערן ? ...

Thunder Struck a Tree ...

Thunder struck a tree.

My soul is a small branch,
On the small branch a small golden bird.

Bird and branch, blood-mingled — —

Where will the wind find a flute?

What bird sing a morning song
Just for the rising sun? ...

טאַנץ איך אַ דבֿקות-טאַנץ ...

טאַנץ איך אַ דבֿקות-טאַנץ
אין שעהען פֿון אומעט,
אין שעהען פֿון ביטול-היש –
פֿון קאַלטן שטילן עצבֿות – –

נעם איך מיך צוזאַמען און גיי אַ דבֿקות-טאַנץ,
אַ חדווה-ריקודל –
אַ טאַנץ
פֿון „נפשי צמאה לך אלהים – –“
אַ טאַנץ
פֿון „כל עצמותי תאמרנה – –“

– – – טאַנץ איך אײַנגעקאָרטשעט,
מיט געפּרעסטע הייסע ברעמען;
אײַנגעפֿלאָכטן,
אײַנגעקנוילט,
מיט פֿאַרמאַכטע פֿעסטע פֿויסטן,
טראָג אין זיי דעם „סוד-הצמצום“ !

טראָג אין מיר דעם „סוד-הצמצום“ !

– – – טאַנץ איך
מיט אויפֿגעריסענע פֿלאַמען-אויגן,
מיט צעפּראַלטע פֿליגל-אָרעמס –
טאַנץ איך קעגן „תּפֿארת שבתּפֿארת“
קעגן שכינה הקדושה –
אַ חסידים-ראָד קעגן שכינה הקדושה
מיט צעכראַסטעט אָפֿן האַרץ –

אַ חסידים-ראָד, –
אַ דבֿקות-טאַנץ !

טאַנץ איך מײַן דבֿקות-טאַנץ
מיט צעכראַסטעט אָפֿן האַרץ – – –

I Dance a God-dazed Dance*

I dance a God-dazed dance
In hours of melancholy,
In hours of self-annihilation —
And cold silent sadness — —

I put myself together and do a God-clung dance,
A little bliss-dance —
A dance
Of "My soul thirsting for you, O God — —"
A dance
Of "All my bones will speak — —"

— — — I dance whorled into myself,
My temples pulsing hot;
I dance root-entangled,
Wool-embrambled,
With clench-tight fists,
Holding inside the secret of divine contraction!

Holding within me the secret of divine contraction!

— — — I dance
With wide-open flaming eyes,
With flayed-out wing-wide arms —
I dance toward the "Beauty Within Beauty",
Toward God's holy Shekhinah —
A hasidic whirl-dance toward the Shekhinah
With an open, dishevelled heart —

A hasidic circle-dance —
A God-whirled dance!

I dance my God-clung dance
With an open dishevelled heart — —

---

*Untitled in the original publication but given there as "Dveykes-tants" (God-dazed dance) on the contents page

בין איך בײַם ברעג שטײן געבליבן ! ...

בין איך בײַם ברעג שטײן געבליבן !
שווימען קאָן איך נישט;
איז קײן לאָטקע פֿאַראַן –

בין איך בײַם ברעג שטײן געבליבן, –
וואַרטן אויפֿן זומער,
טרוקנט ער ס'טײַכל מיר אויס;
וואַרטן אויפֿן ווינטער,
וואַרפֿט ער אַ גלעזערנע בריק מיר אַריבער;
וואַרטן אויפֿן הײליקן,
פֿאַר זײַן שטעקן
לויפֿן וועלן הינטער-ווײַלעכץ צוריק –

בין איך בײַם ברעג שטײן געבליבן –
לערנען וועלן מיך
שווימען פֿון ברעג צו ברעג
און שפּײַען אויף ברעגן;
לערנען פֿישלעך מיך
לעבן און טאָפּיען
און טאַנצן אינעם טאָפּיען;

בין איך בײַם ברעג שטײן געבליבן
און וואַרף מיך אַ בריק
איבער ים און איבער יבשה ...

I Stayed Standing at the Shore ...

I stayed standing at the shore!
I can't swim;
There's no little boat —

I stayed standing at the shore, —
Waiting for summer,
To dry up the little river for me;
Waiting for winter,
To throw a glass bridge over for me;
Waiting for the Holy One,
Waves are running back
Before His rod —

I stayed standing at the shore —
The waves teach me
To swim from shore to shore
And to spit on the shores;
Little fish teach me
To live and to dive
And to dance in the drowning.

I stayed standing at the shore
And I throw myself as a bridge
Across seas and dry land ...

נישט וואַגן זאָל קיינער ...

נישט וואַגן זאָל קיינער
אין מײַן קדשי-קדשים צו קומען,
ווו שאָטנס שוואַרץ בטליתטע,
טוען שטילע עבֿודות,
כּורעים פֿאַלנדיק און שאָרכנדיק.

נישט וואַגן זאָל קיינער
פֿאַר מײַן כּסא-הכּבֿוד צו פֿאַלן,
ווו איך,
אַן אל-רחום-וחנון,
ליג איבער מײַן טרערן-בעקן
און קיל מײַנע הייסע שלעפֿן,
ווו איך,
אַ נוקם ונוטר,
קראַץ די הויט פֿון מײַן לײַב
און מײַנע ווײַסע צבֿאות-לאָקן
ליגן מיר צופֿוסנס ...

נישט וואַגן זאָל קיינער – –

No-One Should Dare ...

No-one should dare
Come into my Holy of Holies,
Where black prayer-shawled shadows
Do silent service
Falling on their knees and rustling.

No-one should dare
To fall before my throne of glory,
Where I,
A God full of mercy and compassion,
Lie stretched over my tear-basin
Cooling my hot temples,
Where I,
Revengeful, vindictive One,
Scratch the skin of my body
And my white Zebaoth curls
Lie at my feet ...

No-one should dare — —

האָב איך אַ ברויט ...

האָב איך אַ ברויט,
אַ בעט,
אַ בוך צום לעזן,
און ווען ס'האַרץ אַװעקצושענקען
האָב איך נישט.

זעץ איך מיך אויפֿן בעט אַנידער,
אין איין האַנט ס'בוך,
אין צווייטע
אַ שטיק ברויט,
און קײַ און לעז,
און קײַ און לעז –
אוי ווען זאָל איך ס'האַרץ אַוועקשענקען ?

זאָל איך אין גאַס אַרויסלויפֿן
און טרעפֿן,
און טרעפֿן ווען ס'איז
און זאָגן אים,
און בעטן אים :
„קום מיט מיר,
קום מיט מיר, –
איך האָב אַ ברויט,
איך האָב אַ בעט,
איך האָב אַ בוך“
און זאָגן :
„איך האָב –
איך האָב
אַ פּולס,
אַ פֿול, פֿול האַרץ;
קום מיט מיר,
קום מיט מיר“ ?

I Have Bread ...

I have bread,
A bed,
A book to read,
But someone to give away my heart to
I haven't.

I sit on the bed,
In one hand the book,
In the other
Some bread,
And I chew and read
And chew and read —
Who shall I give my heart to?

Shall I run out to the street
And somehow divine
And guess who it is
And tell him
And ask him:
"Come with me,
quick, come with me —
I've got bread,
I've got a bed,
I've got a book"
And say:
"I have —
A pulse,
A full full heart
I have; so
Come with me,
Come with me"?

נו,
נו, –
איך פֿלעג דאָך דאָס,
און געטראָפֿן,
און געבעטן,
און געעפֿנט,
און געשענקט ...

נו,
נו, –
איז בלעטערדיקער מײַן האַרץ,
איז אָנגעשריבענער
און פֿולער און פֿולער געוואָרן ...

נו,
נו, –
האָב איך אַ ברויט,
אַ בעט,
אַ בוך;
און מאָרגן,
און איבערמאָרגן,
און אייביק,
און אייביק? – –

Ah,
Well —
I used to after all
And guessed
And asked
And opened
And gave away …

Ah,
Well —
My heart's become more leafed through,
More written out,
Fuller, more full …

Ah,
Well —
So I have
Bread,
A bed,
A book;
And tomorrow
And the day after
And for always
And for ever? …

וואַלדי

אַ גרינע שׂימחה איז אויפֿגעגאַנגען אין מיר
צעקנאָספּעט אין שטראַלן-פּלעטשן –
מײַן יעטוועדער מוסקל,
יעדעס אַטאָם-חלקל
ציטערט פֿאַר שׂימחה.

אַ גרינע שׂימחה איז צעבליט אין מיר !
מיט זון,
מיט בלויען קטורת,
מיט גרינעם צוויטשער בין אין אויסגעפּילט !

צעפּלאָסענע הימלען בלויען אין מיר !
הימלען, לאָנקעס, וואַלדי – – – –
– – – – – – – – – – – –

וואַלדי,
ווי דו, האָב איך אויך געקאָזשלעקעוועט,
געלעקט און אַקעגנגעטאַנצט,
ביז מײַן ליבע,
ביז מײַן שטומע טרײַשאַפֿט
האָט אין מײַנע אַפּלען אויסגעטרוקנט.

וואַלדי,
אויף ווירוואַר-וועגן אויסגעטראָטענע,
זיבן-פֿאַכיק געטורעמטע,
האָב איך אונטער אַספֿאַלט צעגליטן
אַ בלימל געזוכט,
ליבע –
אין אויגן באַברילטע,
און פֿאַר יעדן פֿענסטער
האָט מײַן האַרץ געפּאָכט.

Waldi

A green joy has risen inside me
Wildly-blossoming, ray-babbling —
Each of my muscles,
Each tiny atom-particle
Trembling with joy.

A green joy blossoming within me!
And I'm filled
With sun-warmth,
With blue incense,
With green birdsong!

Wildly-flowing skies are become blue within me!
Skies and pastures, Waldi — — — —
— — — — — — — — — — — —

Waldi,
Like you I turned somersaults,
Licked and danced up to people
Until my love also
And my silent loyalty
Dried up in my eyes.

Waldi,
On confusion-riddled paths,
Once trod seven times,
I too have looked for
The little flower, love,
Under glowing asphalt —
In eye-glass eyes
And in front of every window
My heart was thumping.

ווּאַלדי,
פֿון וואַנען איך קום,
דאָרט פֿאַלן פֿייגעלעך
פֿאַרחלשטע צו דר'ערד,
נאָך אויבן אין הימלען
זיי ווערן פֿאַרטשאַדעט
אין מיטן אַ טרעל,
און אונטן –
אויף ווירבל-וועגן צעגליטע
פֿון פֿאַרחושטע בלאָנדזשער
דערשטיקטע צעטראָטן.

הימלען, לאָנקעס, וואַלדי !
איך בין אַ פֿעלד, אַ גרײַפֿטעס;
אַ ווילדער שמעטערלינג
אַ פֿאַרבן-פֿלאַטערדיקער.
איך בין אַ בלויער פֿויגל
מיט אַ רויטן שנאָבל !

וואַלדי, וואַלדי,
אַ גרינע שׂימחה איז אויפֿגעגאַנגען אין מיר
מײַנע אויגן שפּרודלען ווי דײַנע
שטומע טרײַשאַפֿט
און שטומע ליבע –

איך טאַנץ קעגן לעבן,
איך טאַנץ קעגן וועלט –
אַ שטומע ליבע איז אויפֿגעגאַנגען אין מיר !

Waldi,
Where I come from
Little birds fall
Stricken to the soil,
Still high up there
They are poisoned
In mid-trill,
While down here —
On glowing vertigo-paths
They are trodden-dead by
Confused wanderers.

Skies and pastures, Waldi!
I am a field, a ripe land;
A wild butterfly,
A colour-flutter one.
I am a blue bird
With a red beak!

Waldi, Waldi,
A green joy has risen within me
And my eyes bubble with life like yours:
Silent loyalty
And silent love —

And I dance toward life,
I dance toward the world —
A silent love has risen within me!

דאָס שליסעלע

כ'האָב מיך פֿאַרשלאָסן אין מײַן שטיבל;
כ'האָב מורא פֿאַר מענטשן,
כ'האָב מורא פֿאַר גאַס,
האָב איך די טיר פֿון מײַן שטיבל פֿאַרשלאָסן
פֿאַר לעבן און פֿאַר וועלט –

דעם שליסל דורכן פֿענסטער געוואָרפֿן;

כ'האָב מיך פֿאַרשלאָסן אין מײַן שטיבל,
און דורכן שליסל-לאָך
כ'ישופֿט לעבן און וועלט,
זונות טאַנצן,
שווערדן בלאַנקען,
און לעבן בושעוועט אויף אַלע פֿיר ...

צעשמעטערט איינזאַמקייט די טיר,
לעבן רײַסט די זאַוויאַסעס
און מיט ציין ציט וועלט נ'סקיבל – –

און געפֿירט פֿון זונות צוויי,
מאַרשיר איך דורך,
דורך בושעוועניק צעטאַנצטן לעבן
צווישן שווערדן און האַמער-געבזענט,
צווישן גלאָק און גאָלד-געקלאַנג ...

... אויף אַ מזבח אַן אַלטן,
פֿון כמה דורות שוין אויסגעלאָשענעם,
געפֿינען מיר אַ שליסעלע דאָרט ליגן,
אין אַש פֿון פֿאַרברענטע קרבנות.
און די זונות זאָגן וואָס זײ ווייסן :
ס'איז דאָס שליסעלע פֿונעם גן-עדן-התחתון,
ס'איז דאָס שליסעלע
פֿון בת-מלכּה-פּאַלאַץ מיט זיבן טירן,
ס'איז דער שליסל פֿון יונג-לעבן-טורעם –
און דער מזבח ווערט פֿריש באַגאָסן,
מיט זודיק מענטשן-בלוט.

The Little Key

I locked myself in this little room;
I'm afraid of people,
Afraid of the street outside.
So I locked the door to this little room:
Away from life and the world —

Then I threw the little key out the window!

I locked myself in this little room
And through the key-hole
Life and the world magically enter,
Prostitutes dance,
Swords start glittering
And life rages round on all fours …

Loneliness shatters the door,
Life tears off all its hinges
And with its teeth the world pulls at the hook — —

And led by two prostitutes,
I march through
This raging wildly-dancing life
Between sword and hammer-blow,
Between bell-gong and gold-sound …

… On an altar, an old one,
One extinguished for many generations,
We find a little key still lying there
In the ashes of burnt offerings.
And the prostitutes saying what they know:
It's the little key to the earthly Garden of Eden,
It's the little key
To the Princess-Palace with seven doors,
It's the key for the Young-Life-Tower —
And the altar becomes freshly smeared
With hot human blood.

– – – און איך דערקען דעם שליסל;
ס'איז מייַנער, מייַנער,
פֿון מייַן אויסגעבראָכענעם טירל,
אָן זאַוויאַסעס, אָן סקיבל,
איך דערקען די מייַנע –
ס'איז די שוואַרצע מייַן שוועסטער,
די בלאָנדע מייַן געליבטע,
איך דערקען אַלעס, אַלעס – –
איך טו דעם שליסל אַ קמיעה מיר אָן
און גיי זוכן דעם וועג
צום גן-עדן-התחתון,
צום בת-מלכּה-פּאַלאַץ מיט זיבן טירן,
און זוך דעם וועג
צום יונג-לעבן-טורעם – –

— And I recognise the key;
It is mine, mine,
From my shattered little door
Without hinge or hook.
I recognise my dear ones —
The dark-haired one is my sister,
The blond one my lover.
I recognise everything, everything — —
I put on the key as an amulet
And go to look for the way
To the earthly Garden of Eden,
To the Princess-Palace with seven doors,
And I look for the path
To the Young-Life-Tower — —

אָוונט

קו-קו, קו-קו ! ..
אַן ערשט געבוירן שטערנדל,
פינטלט אין די שטילקייט,
פינטלט,
שוויַגט –

דאָרט צאַפּלט וואָס –
אַ האַרץ ?..
אַ געבונדענע קאַץ ? ..

קו-קו, קו-קו ! ..
אַ פֿאַרשפעטיקטער פֿויגל פֿלאַטערט דורך ...

... אונטער אַן איבערגעוואָרפענעם טלית
שטייט וועלט אַ געבוקטע,
און קלאַפּט
על-חטא, על-חטא,
און ס'פֿאַלט וועלט אין טלית צוזאַמען ...

קו-קו, קו-קו – – – –

Evening

Ku-ku. Ku-ku! ...
A just-been-born little star
Is twinkling in the silence,
Twinkling,
Silent —

Something is quivering there —
A heart? ...
A tied-up cat? ...

Ku-ku. Ku-ku! ...
A belated bird fluttering through ...

... Under its prayer-shawl
The world is standing bowed
And beats its breast
For its sins, its sins,
And breaks down beneath the prayer-shawl ...

Ku-ku. Ku-ku — — —

מעת-לעתן ...

מעת-לעתן,
מעת-לעתן –
ווען איז טאָג,
ווען איז נאַכט ?

אַ בלינדער טורעם אין מיטן שטאָט,
מיט אַ גלאַטן ציפֿערבלאַט – – –
– – – – – – – – – – – – – – –

גלין-גלאָן !
אַ לוויה ?
אַ חופּה ?
גלין-גלאָן ! גלין-גלאָן !
אַז ס'ברענט ?
אַז צו אַ זונטיק-תּפֿילה ?
גלין-גלאָן ! גלאָן-גלין ! גלין-גלאָן ! גלאָן-גלין !
און אַז גאָט ווערט געבוירן – – –

Twenty-Four Hours ...

Twenty-four hours,
Night and day —
When day,
When night?

A blind tower in the centre of the city
With its smooth clock-face — —
— — — — — — — — — — —

Glin-glon!
A funeral?
A wedding?
Glin-glon, glin-glon!
A fire there?
A Sunday prayer?
Glin-glon, glon-glin, glin-glon, glon-glin!
And if God is being born — — —

קריצט אונדזער צײַט ...

קריצט אונדזער צײַט
די מעשׂים אירע,
אויף אויסגעשיילטע מענטשן-בײנער.

לעזנדיק,
וועט דער קומענדיקער דור רונצלען
און מיט פּחד
מישן די בלעטער –

בלעטער פֿון נײַע כּיתבֿי-קודש,
געשריבן אויף אויסגעשיילטע מענטשן-בײנער ...

Our Time Engraves ...

Our time
Engraves its deeds
On bare human bones.

Reading them,
The coming generation will shrivel
And with fear will
Shuffle the pages —

The pages of new holy writings
Written out on bare human bones ...

אויף אַלע בערג ...

אויף אַלע בערג האָב איך ווינטמילן געשטעלט,
אין אַלע טאָלן –
קוואַלן געגראָבן;
דרייען מײַנע מילן –
און מײַן האָבער מיכעצט אומגעדראָשן;
שפּרודלען מײַנע קוואַלן –
און איך שטיי אויף אַלע הויכע בערג
און שרײַ :
וואַסער !
וואַסער !

בערגער דרייען,
טאָלן שפּרודלען,
און מיר שרײַען,
און מיר שרײַען ...

On All the Mountains ...

On all the mountains
I've placed windmills,
Dug source-springs
In all the valleys —
My mills are turning —
But the oats moulder unthreshed;
My springs bubble up —
And I stand on all the high hills
And I scream:
Water!
Water!

Mountains churn,
Valleys bubble up,
And we scream
And we scream …

אַלע מײַנע יונגע יאָרן ...

אַלע מײַנע יונגע יאָרן
זײַנען אַרויס אויפֿן וועג,
וואָס פֿירט צו דיר.

זיי ליגן אײַנגעקאַלכטע מײַלן-שטיינער
אין מיטן וועג –

מיט גרויס אָנגעשריבענע ציפֿערן ! ..

אַלע פֿאַרבײַגייער,
וואָס גייען צו דיר,
קלאַפּן אָן זייערע פֿאַרשטויבטע פֿיס
אין מײַנע ווײַס-געקאַלכטע שטיינער –

בײַ יעדן קלאַפּ
גיט מײַן יונג האַרץ אַ צאַפּל.

אַלע מײַנע יונגע יאָרן
זײַנען אַרויס אויף דײַן וועג,
אַלע מײַנע איבעריקע
גייען באַלאָדנט מיט שווערע שטיינער –

אויף מײַן לעצטן ווײַס-געקאַלכטן
וועט אַ פֿרעמדע האַנט שרײַבן דעם ציפֿער – –

אין מיטן וועג
אונטער מײַן לעצטן ווײַסן שטיין
וועט אייביק צאַפּלען מײַן האַרץ
פֿאַר יעדן פֿאַרבײַגייער,
וואָס גייט צו דיר.

All My Young Years ...

All my young years
Have left on the journey
Towards you.

Like white milestones they are lying
In the middle of the road —

With numbers writ large on them! ...

All passers-by
Who travel toward you
Knock their dusty feet
Against my white miles —

And with each knock
My young heart starts to quiver.

All my young years
Have gone out towards you,
All my remaining years
Will go weighed with heavy stones —

On my final whitened one
A strange hand will write the number — —

In the middle of the road
Under my final white stone
My heart will quiver always
With every passer-by
Who journeys toward you.

פֿון : א.נ. שטענצל, פֿישערדאָרף
(בערלין : ענערגיאַ, 1933)

הויף מיט באָטשאַן

אַ מרוקעוואַטער מרה-שחורהניק
דרייט זיך אַרום אין יעדן הויף אַ פֿערד,
הערט זיך קאַלעמוטנע צו
צו דער שווערער סעטשקע-מאַשין.

וואָרקענדיקע, אַלכסון-בלענדנדיקע רעדער
קומען ווײַסע טויבן געפֿלאַטערט,
אויסגעהונגערטע פֿון פוסטע הימלען,
און וואַקלען, ווי די קאַטשקעס צווישן די וועגענער.

די שטאָדאָלעס, פֿול געפּאַקטע און פֿול געשטאָפּטע,
זײַנען אָפֿענע, פֿולע פּיסקעס;
און פֿון די בלוילעך-ברוינלעך פֿאַרברענטע הימלען
שמעקט עס מיט געבראָטענע באַדעלעס.

בלײַבט עד שטיין, דער גרויסער באָטשאַן
אויף זײַן אויסגעבעטן שטרוידאַך,
הויבט אויף אַ לאַנגן, דאַרן פֿוס
צו זײַן נידעריקער ראיה
און טראַכט צו אַ האַרבלעכן ענין.

From: ***Fisherdorf*** **("Fishing Village")**

Farmyard with Stork

Every farmyard has its horse,
A grumbling, melancholy one
That, as it trudges, listens gloomily
To the heavy chaff-cutting machine.

Like cooing diagonally-dazzling wheels,
White doves come fluttering down,
Come starving out of the empty skies
And waddle about like ducks amid carts.

The barns fully packed and laden
Are wide-opened animal mouths;
And from the bluish-brown burnt skies
Come smells of field-fried potatoes.

The big stork stays standing
On its roof of padded straw
And, lifting a long, thin leg
To its myopic eye,
Reflects on a difficult matter.

ים אין זון

אַ בופֿלאָקס, אַ געשפּיקעוועטער,
אונטער זײַן דיקן, געפֿאַלדעוועטן קאַרק,
גריזשעט ער, דער ים, און זשגײַעט
מיט פֿאַרסלונעטע ווײַסע לעפֿצן.

די פֿעלדזן, זאַפֿטיקע אין זון,
באַוואַקסענע בערג, אַרומגעגריזשעטע,
פֿול צײַטיקער רויטער קלעווער – – –

און אַז דער בויך איז שוין אָן אויסגעפֿרעסענער,
אַן אָפּגעצויגענער, ווי אַ קעסלפּויק,
דרייט ער זיך אויס, דער בופֿלאָקס,
שלעפֿערדיק און גרעפּצנדיק,
צעגלאַנצט אין זײַן געפֿאַלדעוועטער פֿעל,
מיט אַן אויסגעבויגענעם גלאַנצנדיקן רוקן.

Sea in the Sun

A burly, husky buffalo,
Its neck creased below in wrinkle-folds,
The sea nibbles and slurps with
White salivating animal-lips.

Rocks in the juices of the sun,
Overgrown outcrops, nibbled at,
Full of ripe red clover — —

Its belly is already full-blown,
Distended as a kettledrum —
So round it turns, the buffalo,
Sleepy and belching,
Gleaming wildly in its wrinkled folds,
Its back hunched and shiny.

פֿעלדער אין ווינט

געפֿרווירענע פֿאַסטעכער, אויסגעשטרעקטע,
אײַנגעהילטע אין צעריסענע לאַכעס
מיט אַרויסקוקעדיקן הוילן לײַב,
שטייעןביימער, צעשויבערטע,
צווישן תּבֿואה־פֿעלדער, פֿולע און שווערע,
און טרײַבן זיי ווי שעפּסן־סטאַדעס
מיט הייזעריקן „הוי“ און „ווײ“,
אַהיימצוקומען נאָך פֿאַרן געוויטער.

יאָגן די פֿעלדער ווי די ווילדע
מיט דערשראָקענע, פֿאַרשטעקטע קעפּ,
אַרײַנגעדרייט זייערע געדרייטע הערנער
אין פֿאַרפּלאָנטערטע וואָלענע בײַכער,
און זיי שטויסן זיך און פּלאָנטערן זיך,
יאָגן איבער איינע די צווייטע
און פֿאַלן פֿון די פֿאַרמאַטערטע פֿיס — — —

Fields in the Wind

Like frozen shepherds,
Taut and wrapped in torn rags,
With protruding naked patches,
Dishevelled trees are stood there
Amid full and heavy fields of grain.
They drive them like herds of sheep
With a hoarse "hoa" and "whoa",
So as to get home before the storm.

The fields are flailing like wild ones
With their frightened, hidden heads,
Their curly horns curved inwards
And tangled with their belly-wool,
And they push and become entangled,
Push-pulling one with the other
And tripping over their own tired feet —

נאָך דער אַרבעט

אויפֿן שוועל פֿון דער ווײַסער כאַטע
רויכערט ס'פֿויערל זײַן לעצטע פֿײַקע
און וואַרפֿט אַרײַן אַ געציילט וואָרט.
און זײַן אָפּגעאַרבעט פֿערדל אין שטאַל
זופּט גרויסע זופּן
און קראַצט מיט אַ וואַקלדיקער פּאָדקעווע.

ס'ברעכט אַזוי מחיהדיק אין די ביינער,
אַזוי מנוחהדיק גוט,
און דעם הונטס אויפֿגעשטעלטע אויערן
כאַפּן אויף שטיקלעך שמועסן
מכּוחן מאָרגנדיקן וועטער ...

אַפּנים זיי האָבן זייער אײַליק,
די סטאַדעס ווײַסינקע וואָלקנדלעך,
וואָרעם זיי ציִען שנעל אַריבער
איבערן שטילן מידן דאָרף.

After Work

On the doorstep of the white hut
The old farmer smokes a last pipe
And throws in his measured word.
And the weary horse in the stable
Mouths up big sips of water
And scratches with a shaky shoe.

Something burns so joyfully,
So peacefully in those bones,
And the dog's pricked-up ears
Catch little snatches of talk
About tomorrow's weather ...

Seemingly they are in a hurry,
The herds of white little clouds,
Since they pass quickly overhead
Above the exhausted, quiet village.

דער אַלטער פּישער

זײַנע ביינער צעקריכן זיך אונטער זײַן צעאַרבעטעטער הויט,
ליידיקע פּלאַשן וואָס ליגן אין אַ שמאָלן זאַק.
און די באַקן-ביינער און די ביעדרעס
סטאַרטשען שוין ווי צעבראָכענע שאַרבנס.

זײַן אײַנגעפּאַלן מויל איז צוזאַמענגעצויגן
ווי דער טאַבעק-בײַטל וואָס זי האָט אים נאָך אויפֿגענייט :
העה-העה-העה ! בײַ יעדן שיף האָט זי אים אָפּגעוואַרט
און יעצט וואַרט זי אים דרויסן אָפּ בײַ יעדן אַרויסגעברענגטן.

ער אָבער לייענט נאָך אַלץ די וועטערס פֿון די הימלען
און זיצט אײַנגעפּאַלן פֿאַרן שיפּער-הײַזל,
אַ צוגעשרויפּטער אויף אַלע פּיר,
ווי דער מאַנאָמעטער פֿאַרן מעשענעם קעסל.

און רייניקנדיק די נעצן פֿון מושלען און גרעזער
נאָגט ער נאָך אַלץ ווי פֿאַר אַכציק יאָר,
ווען ער האָט געזויגן דאָס צוקער-שמאַטקעלע,
דעם שמייכל פֿון זײַן אײַנגעפּאַלענעם מויל.

The Old Fisherman

His bones mapped beneath exhausted skin
Like empty bottles lining a tiny sack.
And his cheek-bones and his ribs
Already sticking out like broken shards.

His sunken mouth is pulled tight
Like the little tobacco-pouch she'd sewn him:
Hoi! Hoi! She's waited for him with each incoming boat
And now she waits outside where they bring the dead.

He still reads the weather from the skies
And sits sunken in front of the small cabin —
It seems he's screwed-down on all fours:
A pressure-gauge with a brass-kettle.

And cleaning nets of mussels and weed
He chews once again as he did eighty years ago
When he sucked on his child's sugar-cloth,
Smiling from his sunken mouth.

די באַלאַדע פֿון דער באָרעווקע-באָבע

אַרויסגעריסענע קושאַקעס מיט וואָרצלען
זעען אויס אירע אויסגעטריקנטע הענט.
און די באָרעווקעס וואָס זי מעסט אָן
זײַנען זיכער די אַרויסגערינענע בלוט-טראָפּן.

ווען זי איז אַ יונג בלוט געווען,
האָט זי שוין אירע ערשטע מילך פֿאַרקויפֿט אין שטאָט,
יענער, וואָס האָט איר דעם בויך געמאַכט,
האָט זי אַהינגעפֿירט ווי אַ פֿולע מילך-קאַן !

און איצט נאָך, ווען זי רעדט, קומט עס אַרויס פֿון איר,
אַן אַרויסגאָרגלדיקער איבערגעבליבענער שלונג – –
אַ בלעכענע מילך-קאַן אַ צעבויגענע,
שטייט זי אַזוי מיט אירע אײַנגעפֿאַלענע באַקן.

The Ballad of the Bilberry Seller

Like shrubs with torn-out roots:
Her dried-up hands resemble this.
And the bilberries that she's weighing
Are surely drops of dripping blood.

When she was still a blood-young girl
She'd already sold her first milk in town,
The one who had made her belly big
Led her there full as a frothing churn!

Still now when she talks it bursts out:
A gargled left-over gullet-full — —
A tin milk-churn, a dented bent one —
She stands there with sunken cheeks.

דאָס שטורעם-ליד

אַ קאַץ מיט גרינע אויגן פֿאַרזשמורעטע,
מיט אײַנגעצויגענע שאַרפֿע גראַטשעס,
איז דער גרויסער אָקעאַן אין זון,
אײַנדרימלענדיק ברומט ער פֿון צעוואַרעמטן בויך אַרויס !

האָ, האָ, האָ, מיר זײַנען קיין מײַז נישט,
מיר צעלויפֿן זיך נישט ווי די ראַטן אין שיף,
ווען די קאַץ לייגט זיך אויפֿן שפּרונג,
מיט שפּריצנדיקע, לויפֿנדיקע וואָנסעס !

האָ, האָ, האָ, מיר זײַנען קיין מײַז נישט !
מיט זעגל-שטריק בינדן מיר אירע לאַפּעס !
און קוקנדיק אין אירע אויגן אירע גרינע,
זינגען מיר פֿון ווײַבער, פֿון קעצישע !

האָ, האָ, האָ, פֿעסטער געצויגן, פֿעסטער !
אין האַפֿן וואַרטן ווײַבער אויף אונדז
מיט וואַרעמע בײַכער ווי קעצישע פֿעל
און בראָנפֿן אין בײַכיקע, גרויסע פֿעסער !

Storm-Song

The ocean big in the sun is like
A cat with green squinting eyes
And with pulled-in sharp claws,
Dozily rumbling from her warm belly!

Ha, Ha, Ha! We are not mice,
We don’t run off like rats in a ship
When cat lies waiting to pounce
With trembling expectant whiskers!

Ha, Ha, Ha! We are not mice!
With sail-ropes we bind up her paws!
And looking right into her green eyes
We sing of women, of cat-like ones!

Ha, Ha, Ha! Pull tighter still!
In the port women are waiting for us,
With warm bellies like cat’s fur and with
Brandy sloshing round in big barrels!

רחבֿות און רו און לויטערקייט ...

רחבֿות און רו און לויטערקייט – –
פֿלאַטערן פֿאַרזילבערטע
פֿאַלן מעוועס אין רוישיקע וועלן
ווי שטערן אין סוף-זומערנעכט –
וואָס נאָך קאָן איך מיר ווינטשן ?!

אַ טאָג הענגט זאַפּטיק איבער מײַן קאָפּ,
אַ צײַטיקער רויטער עפּל – –
כ'וועל אים אַרונטעררײַסן,
אים אָפּשיילן ווײַס און יאָדערדיק,
און וואַרפֿן זײַן שאָלעכץ הינטער מיר.

רחבֿות און רו און לויטערקייט – –
אין פֿאַרגילדעטן שפּע-געציטער
שלענגלט עס זיך דורכזעעוודיק און דין :
„ס'וועלן מעוועס פֿאַלן איבער דיר
ווי שטערן אין אַ סוף-זומערנאַכט“.

Spaciousness and Quiet and Lucidity

Spaciousness and quiet and lucidity — —
Fluttering, silvery
Seagulls fall into the roaring waves
Like stars in late summer nights —
What else could I wish for myself?!

Day hangs juicily about my head
Like a ripe and full-red apple — —
I will pluck it off,
Peel it until it's white and pithy
And throw the peel away behind me.

Spaciousness and quiet and lucidity — —
In gold-rimmed plenty-trembling,
It goes winding, transparently, thin:
"Seagulls will fall from above you
Like stars in a late summer's night."

אויף דער לאָנקע

ווי פֿון אַ פֿולן איבערגייענדיקן עמער
און ווי פֿון אַלע זײַנע ביינער
גיסט עס זיך ווי פֿון אַלע זײַטן,
אַ וואַרעמקייט און אַ ליכטיקייט.

ווי פֿון זיך אַליין
הויבן זיך די שווערע, קלעפּיקע לעפּלעך !
עס ווילט זיך אים גוט זײַן,
דעם געפּענטעטן פֿאַרתּמטן פֿערד,
לייגט ער אַרויף זײַן וואַרעמען האַלדז
אויף אַ צווייטן פֿערדישן האַלדז.

שטייען זיי ביידע,
צוויי געפּענטעטע פֿאַרתּמטע פֿערד,
וואָס זײַנען זיך געפֿאַלן אויף די העלדזער,
מיט ליכטיקע אָפֿענע אויגן,

און זייער ביידנס וואַרעם בלוט
גיסט זיך דורך זיי,
פֿליסנדיק אין איין עמער.

In the Meadows

As from a bucket rising past its rim
And as if from all its horse-bones,
From all sides it floods over
With warmth and lucid light.

As if on their own
Its heavy, sticky ears perk up!
And it wants to be at ease,
This tethered simple horse,
And lays its warm neck
Against another's.

So they stand there together,
Two tethered simpleton-horses,
Fallen on each other's necks
With lucid, open eyes.

And the warm blood of them
Flows right through them both
Flooding into one bucket.

אויפֿן ים

אַ ווינט און אַ רעגן,
וויַסע באָרוועסע קאַטשקעלעך
באָדן זיך די כוואַליעס –
צערעווען מיט די פֿיסלעך
די לעכער אין די וואָלקנס – – –

געוואַלטיק איז דער ים, ווען ער שטורעמט,
אַ האַרץ אָבער איז גרויס,
ווען ס'קאָן שטיל זיַין – – –
– – – – – – – – – – – – –
און דער ים לאָזט זיך באַקוקן
ווי אַ קינד, וואָס פּליטשקעט מיט די פֿיסעלעך.

On the Sea

Wind and rain,
Like white barefoot little ducks
The waves take a bath —
Darning with their tiny feet
The holes in the clouds — — —

The sea swells heavily when it storms,
But a heart can be great
When it is calm — — —
— — — — — — — — — —
And the sea allows itself to be gazed on
Like a child that's splashing its feet …

בענקשאַפֿט

איבער אַ סטרויענדיקן באַס
מיט אָנגעצויגענע, גראָבע סטרונעס,
אַ האַנט מיט אויסגעצערטע צאַרטע פֿינגער,
גייט די לאָטקע אונטן מיט די מאַסטן
צווישן די ברומענדיקע כוואַליעס.

אין גאַנצן זעט ער אויס, דער ים,
אַן אויסגעצויגענע האַרמאָניקע,
און יענער, וואָס האַלט זי אויף דעם שויס,
דריקט שוין אויף די ווײַסע קלאַווישן,
גרייט אַרײַנצופֿאַלן מיט הויכע טענער.

און הויקערדיק און שאָטנדיק,
אונטער די צעפֿאָכעטע ווערבע, הינטן,
שנײַדט ווער זיך אַ פֿרישינקע צווײַגל,
אויסצופֿײַפֿן דעם פֿאַרשוויגענעם טרויער
פֿון געפֿעלדעלטע צוקנדיקע ליפּן.

Longing

As above a bass being tuned —
Its thick strings tensely-plucked —
By a hand with exhaustion-thinned tender fingers,
A little boat moves, down there, with its masts
Among the roaring waves.

The sea looks like nothing
So much as a fully extended accordion,
And the one who holds it on his lap
Is already pressing the white keys
Ready to fall in with the high notes.

Hunchbacked and shadowy,
Beneath and behind the wind-fanned willow
Somebody's cutting a fresh switch for himself,
So as to whistle out the silent sadness
From puckered twitching lips.

איר אײַנגערעמט פּאָרטרעט

לײַכט און ווייך און שטיל
מיט געציטער פֿון שאָרכנדיקע וויעס
איבער גאָלד פֿון צײַטיקע זאַנגען
שוועבט איר שמאָל-פּנימדיקער קאָפּ –
ווי אײַנגעראָמט זעט ער אויס
און אויף בלאָען טיפֿן הינטערגרונט.

די צוויי דינע ליפּן,
שאַרפֿע און טונקל-צונויפֿגעביסן,
זײַנען אַזוי שטיל,
אַ סך, אַ סך שטילער
פֿון די שלאָפֿנדיקע, שטילע ליפּן
פֿון דער אונטערגעגאַנגענער זון,
וואָס רוען ווייך און טונקל
אויף די גלאַטע, שטילע כוואַליעס.

Her Framed Portrait

Light and soft and still
With a tremble of rustling lashes
Above the gold of ripe sheaves,
Her thin-faced head hovers —
It looks as if it's framed there
On a blue deep background.

Her two thin lips,
Sharp and darkly bitten together,
Are so still,
So much more still
Than the sleeping still lips
Of the sun that's set,
Resting soft and dark
On smooth, still waves.

בין־השמשות־ווינטל

שלעפֿעריקע פֿליגעלעך
פֿאָכן אויס זייערע פֿעדערן,
ציִען אײַן זייערע שלעפֿעריקע קעפּלעך.

האַלב שוין אײַנגעשלעפֿערטע,
געררויטלט אין וואַכיקן שעפּטשען – –
ווײַסע געשיילטע בעריאָזקעלעך.

און אַ גרויסער שטויביקער זונען־בלום
באַוועגט זיך שווער און טונקל,
ווי אַן אויפֿגייענדיקע פֿולע לבֿנה.

A Light Twilight Wind

Sleepy tiny bird-wings
Fan out their feathers
And pull in tired little heads.

Already half-asleep
And reddened with soft whispering — —
White peeled little birch trees.

And a big, dusty sunflower
Swaying heavily and dark
Like a full, rising moon.

שקיעה

פֿון אַלע מײַנע גלידער וואַקסט פֿינסטערניש,
אונטערגייענדיקע שיפֿן
הענגען שטאַנגען אַרויס מיט שוואַרצע פֿענער –

אין יעדן בלוט-טראָפּן
ברעכן זיי צוזאַמען,
צוזאַמענגעשטויסענע, צעשמעטערטע – – –

ברעכט אויף מײַנע אויגן !
בלוי און בליציק דורך ברויזנדיק שוואַרץ,
אויפֿגעלויכטענע סיגנאַלן !

Sunset

Out of my limbs darkness grows,
Sinking ships
Flail out poles of black flags —

In every drop of blood,
Collapsed in on themselves,
Colliding ones, crushed ones — — —

Shatter open, my eyes!
Blue and flashed through sparkling black,
Flared-out signals!

לײַכט־טורעם

אַ גײיענדיקער װינטמיל אין מיטאָג־זון,
מיט אַלע אירע שפּרײַזן אַ צעשטראַלטע,
אַזוי זעט אויס דער לײַכט־טורעם,
אויפֿגעלויכטן אין מיטן דער פֿינסטערניש !
און דאָס כּסדרדיקע רוישן און שוימען,
איז דאָס צערײַבן װערן פֿון די קערנער !

און ערד דו, װאָס ביסטו,
ביסטו דער שװערער מילשטײן אפֿשר,
אונטער װעלכן מיר קומען אַרונטער ?
און דאָס כּסדרדיקע שוימען און רוישן,
דאָס צערײַבן זיך אונדזערע אַלעמענס בײנער ?
ערד דו, אויפֿגעלויכטן מיט אַלע אונדזערע לעבנס ...

Lighthouse

A working windmill in the midday sun
With all of its wooden spars flared out,
This is what the lighthouse looks like,
Lit up in the midst of the dark!
And the constant soughing and foaming
Is the grain being crushed around!

And you Earth, what are you?
Just perhaps the heavy millstone
Beneath which we are ground?
And the constant foaming and soughing
Our bones all crushed together here?
You Earth lit up with all our lives …

נאַכט-תּפֿילה

„ווי צוויי מאָן-בלומען, וואָס שטייען אין שכנות
און שליסן זיך אין דער פֿאַרנאַכט-שעה,
און בויגן זיך שטיל און עניוותדיק,
יעדע פֿאַרשלאָסן אין זיך,
יעדע פֿאַרטיפֿט אין זיך,
אַזוי וועלן מיר זיך בויגן שטיל און עניוותדיק,
יעדער פֿאַרשלאָסן מיט זיך,
יעדער פֿאַרטיפֿט אין זיך — — —
ווײַל אַ טיילכל פֿון איין שטראַל
איז געפֿאַלן אין אונדזערע ביידנס הערצער.“

Night-Prayer

"Like two poppies standing together
That close up in the hour of dusk
And bow down quietly and humbly,
Each enclosed in itself,
Each engrossed in itself,
We will bow down quietly and humbly,
Enclosed in our own selves,
Engrossed in our own selves — — —
Because a small part of one beam of light
Has fallen into both of our hearts."

Bibliography

1. Stencl's works from his German period

A. Editions in Yiddish:

In oyfgeyn, tragedye (Rising, tragedy), Leipzig: M. Kleinman Farlag, 1922.

Lider un gedikhtn (Shorter and longer verse), Leipzig, Menes Farlag, 1924.

Un du bist Got (And you are God), Leipzig: Shemesh Farlag, 1925.

Zukh ikh dikh. Libe-lider (I seek you. Love poems), Leipzig: Shemesh Farlag, 1925.

32. In Darser vald baym yam. (32. In the forest of Darss by the sea), Berlin: Energiadruk, 1933.

Fisherdorf (Fishing village), Berlin: Farlag un drukeray "Energia". 1933.

Mayn fisherdorf (My fishing village), Berlin: Fürst, 1935.

Mazl tole (The Sign of the Ram), Berlin: Fürst, 1935.

Fundervaytns (From afar), Berlin: Fürst, 1935.

Oyfn rog (On the corner), Berlin: Fürst, 1935.

Tsvishn himl un erd (Between heaven and earth), Berlin: Rubin Mas, 1936.

Funderheym (From home), Berlin: Fürst, 1936.

Mendele Moykher Sforim, Berlin: Fürst, 1936.

B. Editions in German translation:

Fischerdorf, (Fishing village) translated by Etta Federn-Kohlhaas, Berlin-Wilmersdorf: Kartell Lyrischer Autoren, 1931.

Ring des Saturn (Ring of Saturn), translated by E. Wöhler, Berlin: Rabenpresse, V.O. Stomps, 1932.

2. Literature on A.N. Stencl:

Grossman, Jeffrey, “Farvos ignorirn di literatur-historiker A.N. Shtentslen?” (Why do the literary historians ignore A.N. Stencl?) In: *Oksforder yidish, A Yearbook of Yiddish Studies.* Vol. 1, ed. Dovid Katz, London: Harwood Academic Publishers, 1990, pp. 91-106.

Katz, Dovid, “Stencl of Whitechapel.” *The Mendele Review,* vol. 7, no. 3, 30 March 2003.

http://www2.trincoll.edu/~mendele/tmrarc.htm

Leksikon fun der nayer yidisher literatur (Lexicon of Modern Yiddish Literature), [8 volumes] New York: Congress for Jewish Culture, vol. 8 (1981), pp. 643-4.

Prawer, S.S., *A.N. Stencl, Poet of Whitechapel,* Oxford: Oxford Centre for Postgraduate Hebrew Studies, 1984.

Valencia, Heather, *Else Lasker-Schüler und Abraham Nochem Stenzel. Eine unbekannte Freundschaft* (Frankfurt am Main — New York: Campus Verlag) 1995.

Valencia, Heather, “Czeladz, Berlin and Whitechapel: the world of Abraham Nokhem Stencl”. *European Judaism,* vol 1, 1997, pp. 4-13.

Valencia, Heather, “Dieser erstaunliche Jude”: Abraham Nochem Stenzels Berliner Jahre. Renate Heuer (Hg): *Verborgene Lesarten. Neue Interpretationen deutsch-jüdischer Texte von Heine bis Rosenzweig.* Frankfurt/New York: Campus Verlag 2003 (Reihe Campus Judaica, Bd 20) S. 203-221, Anhang Fischerdorf, S. 222-229.

3. Literature on Eastern European Jews in Weimar Germany:

Aschheim, Steven E., "The East European Jew and German Jewish Identity", in *Studies in Contemporary Jewry*, vol. 1, Bloomington: Indiana University Press, 1984, pp. 3-25.

Aschheim, Steven E., *Brothers and Strangers. The East European Jew in German and German-Jewish Consciousness.* Madison, London: University of Wisconsin Press, 1982.

Charney, Daniel, *A yortsendlik aza* (Such a decade), New York: Tsiko Farlag, 1943.

Charney, Daniel, *Di velt iz kaylekhdik* (The world is round), Tel Aviv, 1963.

Fuks, L. and Fuks, R., "Yiddish Publishing Activities in the Weimar Republic, 1920-1933", in: *Leo Baeck Institute Yearbook*, London, 1988, pp. 417-434.

Gay, Peter, *Freud, Jews and other Germans,* New York: Oxford U.P., 1978, p. 110.

Levine, Glenn, "Yiddish Publishing Activities in Berlin and the Crisis in Eastern European Jewish Culture," in: *Leo Baeck Institute Yearbook* 42, 1997, pp. 85-108.

Maurer, Trude, "The East European Jew in the Weimar Press: Stereotype and Attempted Rebuttal," in: *Studies in Contemporary Jewry,* vol 1, Bloomington: Indiana University Press, 1984, pp. 176-198.

Translators' Notes

The poems presented here are taken from two collections of A.N. Stencl's poetry: *Un du bist Got* (And you are God), 1925, and *Fisherdorf* (Fishing Village), 1933. Stencl's orthography and grammar in these collections are very different from modern standard Yiddish, and he uses several rather unusual words, partly based on his own very rare dialect, spoken in the region of Częstochowa. In the Yiddish text, Stencl's orthography has been standardised in order to make the text more accessible to modern Yiddish readers, particularly students of Yiddish. Thus the Yiddish text presented here employs the standard YIVO orthography, used by Uriel Weinreich in his *Modern English-Yiddish Yiddish-English Dictionary* (New York: McGraw-Hill, 1968). But neither Stencl's grammar, nor his dialectal words, nor his own specific forms of words have been altered, in order to give the reader a flavour of the poet's own stylistic idiosyncracies.

In the English text, the standard YIVO transliteration has been used for Yiddish names, except where there is an alternative conventional spelling of a Yiddish name e.g. Daniel Charney, not *Danyel Tsharni*. Similarly, the normal Polish spelling of place names in Poland is given, rather than their Yiddish equivalents, e.g. Częstochowa instead of the Yiddish *Tshenstokhov*.

In the book, Stencl's name appears in several different forms: he himself used the Polish spelling "Stencl", when writing in Roman letters, so that his name, when used in an English context is written Avrom Nokhem (Avram Nuchem) Stencl, or more usually A.N. Stencl, as he always signed himself. In German he is usually known as "Abraham Nochem Stenzel", and this spelling is used in the German context.

The term for "fishing village" is the same in both Yiddish and German, but is spelt "Fisherdorf" when referring to the Yiddish text, and "Fischerdorf" for the German version of the work.

HBW and HV

Moving to Whitechapel when I (Stephen Watts) was in my early twenties – this was in the mid-1970's — I used to see four or five old men huddled round a table at the very back of the ABC Café opposite the London Hospital. I guessed they were speaking Yiddish but I didn't know who they were. One of them — I realised in retrospect — must have been Avrom Stencl. As I came to know more of him after his death — through the few articles and obituaries that were in English, and from talking to friends such as Bill Fishman and Chaim Neslen and Rachel Lichtenstein — the idea of a book of Stencl poems in English started to form. Nothing happened however until Haike Beruriah Wiegand and I met at "Friends of Yiddish" in 2003, when we decided to try and translate a few poems. We carried on and these co-translations from the poems of Stencl's Berlin years are part of what we've done.

Haike Beruriah Wiegand (herself a poet writing in Yiddish) first provided a close literal version, which we both worked on together. Stephen Watts then took these worked literals and tried to bring them closer to "finished" English poems. We then both scrutinised what we had done and reworked them back and forth until we were more or less satisfied with what we had.

We have tried to retain the qualities of the Yiddish, its freshness and its strangenesses: to this end we have attempted to find a balance that adheres to the literal meaning while at the same time risking an equivalence that provides a good poem in English. Both have seemed equally important to us and we hope that we have not strayed too far from either.

We felt very fortunate in having as good a Stencl scholar and friend as Heather Valencia to bounce our work off and comment on its accuracy, and as knowledgeable a Yiddish scholar as Yitskhok Niborski to confer with over the difficulties of Stencl's language and the orthography of the Yiddish text. We would like to thank both Heather Valencia and Yitskhok Niborski for their help and encouragement, also our publisher Ross Bradshaw.

Haike Beruriah Wiegand would also like to thank Ray Willmott for his help and support. We would like to dedicate this book to the memory of Majer Bogdanski (1912-2005), Stencl's friend and colleague and chair of "Friends of Yiddish" for many years after Stencl's death.

HBW & SW

Stencl in London

Writing in 1965, Bill Fishman, the leading chronicler of London's East End wrote of Whitechapel as being a "dying ghetto" where "A few mumbling ancients remain as the depositors of its sadness and glory." He pointed out that there was a breath of continuity, as "Avraham Stencl still sings the songs of his people."

Writing in *ELAM* (Winter 1965) Bill Fishman said of Stencl: "His presence is convincing: of medium height in his shabby brown suit he has the stooping shoulders of the Talmudic scholar. His features vitalise the frame. Intense blue eyes under once-fair greying hair; a small hawk nose brooding over full lips and a square jaw; the traditional gesticulations for emphasis and a quick change of expression from an almost beatific smile to mild anger provoked by any sign of flattery... He was born in a small mining town in Poland, and one of his earliest memories [was] when he was six. He remembered: 'Curiosity led me to hide in my uncle's wagon behind a huge mass of loaves collected by him to give to the women-folk waiting at the pit head. It was unforgettable for me as well as for them. I helped to distribute the loaves, and their men never came back.'"

Yet Stencl was reticent about his early life, saying only of Germany "I loved the country, and I walked and talked with philosophers and poets of all faiths. Then came Hitler with his storm and hatred. That is all I want to remember now..." And then came Whitechapel.

Stencl told Fishman that, by the 60s he travelled "...from *shul* to *shul* but cannot find spiritual peace. Years ago in the poor little shabby *stiebels* (prayer-houses) of the Chassidim, there I heard the people talk to God." And talking again of Whitechapel he said: "I feel lost, especially with the going of the Workers' Circle. I still love Whitechapel because here was the centre of salvation for thousands of Jews who came fleeing from hatred and persecution. There were 60,000 Jewish workers when I first came and I was proud to be amongst them... This and London soon stimulated me to write afresh. At this sprawling mass of ten million people co-existing in peaceful tolerance... Its freedom — its lyricism is no less incomprehensible to me than the wonder of Shakespeare."

Stencl added "I still get sustenance from the shrill bright life of the Whitechapel Waste, especially the blazing stalls on Friday market night. This perpetually fills me with the beauty of the Sabbath coming in as radiant as a bride."

Bill Fishman concluded the interview in *ELAM* by remarking on the significance of Stencl then. He wrote: "[Stencl], in his imagination, has willed away the final dissolution of his people. In his dying *mame loshen* he recreates with pathos and with dignity a yesterday which is alive and vivid to him now as it was then. For he is the last of the dreamers of the ghetto..."

Uncle Avram

Avram Nuchem Stencl was always "uncle" to me. He was in fact my father's uncle (his father's only sibling), but as there was only 10 years between them, they were very close. He was also the only relative I had in Britain, apart from my parents, so he was just always part of my growing up.

I was brought up in Stamford Hill, in an Orthodox home, and as he lived in the East End, just a bus ride away, he would frequently come to our house to visit us. My memories are mainly from the late fifties and sixties, when Yiddish in the East End was diminishing. He would enjoy coming to Stamford Hill and seeing the little Chassidish children with their long curly *peyes* conversing in Yiddish. He would always stop and have a short chat with them.

He always arrived unannounced, but always with a box of chocolates or some other goodies. He used to come about once a fortnight, but we never knew when he would come. He would always join us for Jewish festivals, *seder* nights, and always when it was one of the families' *yahrzeits*. Best of all was Chanukah, when he always turned up with eight coins for Chanukah *gelt* and a bag of nuts to play *dreidel*. This must have been a nostalgia trip to his childhood as he was not a strictly observant man at this stage of his life.

Whenever he came, he would empty out of his pocket the reams of continuous paper on which he wrote his poetry and read them to my father for correction. My father had been a political journalist, but was quite ill with Parkinson's Disease at this time and unable to work. I think that he enjoyed being consulted about Avram Nuchem's work, and could help with the grammar and spelling, but I think that the artistic detail was beyond him.

As my father was ill, Avram Nuchem would try to give me treats and take me on outings. I remember many trips to Westcliffe by train and a lunch at the kosher boarding house there. He would scribble and write his poems on the journeys and thoroughly enjoy his day out walking alongside the beach or on the pier. I also remember a visit to the National Gallery. He took me round quite a few of the rooms introducing me to the artists, but did insist that a large number of the portraits had "Jewish" faces. He always bought me postcard presents of my favourite pictures.

When I first met my husband to be and brought him home, he must have thought he was in a foreign country. Yiddish or German were the languages in the house and my uncle refused to speak anything else. There is a story that he was once sent to a remote English village to learn English, but instead of Avram Nuchem learning English the villagers were learning Yiddish.

Avram Nuchem was always consulted about my education. My parents wanted a narrow Jewish education, but thanks to Avram Nuchem's advice I was allowed both a grammar school education and the opportunity to go to university. He was very determined that I should achieve my potential and going to university was a big decision for a *frum* girl in the sixties. He must have felt quite responsible about this decision as he turned up at the station to see me off for my first term at Manchester University.

As has already been written by other writers, his clothes were a very low priority and he wore second-hand scruffy clothes with bulging pockets most of the time. As my father was in a wheelchair at the time of my wedding, it fell upon Avram Nuchem to walk me down the aisle. For several weeks before the wedding, there was much discussion as to what he would wear. He was adamant that there was no way that he would wear the customary dinner suit and top hat that was the custom of the day in the late sixties. On the morning of the wedding he arrived at my house in his usual well worn overcoat, but when he removed his coat, there he was dressed in a hired dinner suit. He certainly looked very smart and said that he had not wanted to spoil the very nice atmosphere that existed between the two families.

Sadly, I saw less of him when I moved to Manchester, but he always came round when I returned to London to visit my parents. The last time I saw him was when he was in a nursing home and quite ill.

Miriam Becker